HIGH TECH ARCHITECTURE

HIGH TECH ARCHITECTURE
COLIN DAVIES

with 342 illustrations, 81 in colour

THAMES AND HUDSON

First published in Great Britain in 1988 by
Thames and Hudson Ltd, London

Printed and bound in West Germany

Contents

High Tech – A tentative definition

High Tech architects all agree on at least one thing: they hate the term "High Tech". Apart from a natural human unwillingness to be pigeonholed, there seem to be three main reasons for this.

The first is that in the early 1970s "High Tech" was often used as a term of abuse by architects who had taken up the fashionable cause of "alternative technology". As the term passed into more general use it lost its negative connotations, but High Tech architects themselves still prefer to use some such phrase as "appropriate technology". Second, it is an ambiguous term. High Tech in architecture means something different from High Tech in industry. In industry, it means electronics, computers, silicon chips, robots, and the like; in architecture it now means a particular *style* of building.

But as soon as we use the word style we come up against the third objection. British High Tech architects hate the word style even more than they hate the words High Tech. In the USA the term High Tech does refer mainly to a style, but in Britain it means something much more rigorous. It is High Tech in the British sense that this book sets out to analyse and illustrate. It is too late now to invent a new name. Most people interested in contemporary architecture know what High Tech means, at least in general terms. And if High Tech has nothing to do with high technology, well neither has Gothic anything to do with Goths.

So exactly what does it mean? The physical and ideological features of High Tech are analysed in some detail in the pages that follow. For now we can simply say that its characteristic materials are metal and glass, that it purports to adhere to a strict code of honesty of expression, that it usually embodies ideas about industrial production, that it uses industries other than the building industry as sources both of technology and of imagery, and that it puts a high priority on flexibility of use.

It could, alternatively, be defined in purely personal and historical terms as the label we apply to almost any building designed in the last twenty years by Richard Rogers, Norman Foster, Nicholas Grimshaw, or Michael Hopkins. There are other exponents of High Tech, and not all of them are British, but these four are the leaders of the movement. And it is, in a sense, a movement. It holds no conferences and issues no manifestos, but most of its members share the same educational background and are known personally to one another. They have worked in each other's offices, and exchange ideas, sometimes collaborating, sometimes competing.

A number of theories have been put forward as to why this style of building should have developed in Britain rather than, say, Germany, America, or Japan. Perhaps it is nostalgia for the great days when the Empire was serviced and maintained as much by engineers as by industrialists, politicians, and generals.[1] Perhaps it is a continuation of the tradition of Pugin, who demanded "that there should be no features about a building which are not necessary for convenience, construction or propriety" and "that all ornament should consist of the essential construction of the building."[2] Perhaps it follows from the British professional tradition that requires architects to concern themselves with, and be responsible for, the technical details as well as the spaces, forms, and surfaces of their buildings. Or perhaps it is merely a reflection of that British literal-mindedness that sees architecture not as high-flown art or philosophy, but first and foremost as technique. Perhaps, perhaps not. They are only theories, yet there is something indefinably British about High Tech.

Function and representation – Technique or style?

The exponents of High Tech, like the pioneer Modernists of the 1920s, believe that there is such a thing as the "spirit of the age" and that architecture has a moral duty to express that spirit. The spirit of our age, according to High Tech architects, resides in advanced technology. Architecture must therefore participate in and make use of that technology – the technology of industry, transport, communication, flight, and space travel. Why, they ask, should buildings be any different from the other artifacts of industrial culture? Why do we continue to make buildings out of cumbersome, messy, imprecise materials such as bricks, mortar, concrete, and timber when we could be making them out of light, precision components of metal and glass, fabricated in factories and quickly bolted together on site?

The High Tech architect sees architecture as a branch of industrial technology. He claims no social or artistic privileges. He wishes his buildings to be judged by the same criteria of performance as any of the other tools of everyday life. He wants them to be functional and efficient, not artistic or symbolic.

But there is an ambiguity here. Architecture, it seems, can never be purely functional, no matter how hard it tries. The typical High Tech building symbolizes and represents technology rather than simply using it in the most efficient way possible. It may be cheaper and quicker to build a load-bearing brick wall, but the High Tech architect will always prefer the steel frame and the lightweight metal panel because this is a technique more in tune with the spirit of the age. He is committed to the idea that building must eventually catch up with the rest of technology, and he is determined to "drag building into the twentieth century". In this endeavour, symbolism and representation have an important part to play. The motifs of High Tech – exposed steel structure, visible air conditioning ducts, plug-in service pods, and so on – are almost never the most economical solutions. There is nearly always a cheaper, more practical alternative. But this is architecture, not engineering.

High Tech architecture, then, is not purely functional. But neither is it purely representational. It is an article of the High Tech faith that there must be a functional justification for every design decision. Take, for example, the tension structure of Nicholas Grimshaw's Ice Rink in Oxford (page 94). It converts a straightforward, shed-like building into a dynamic, self-advertising, instantly identifiable piece of architecture that irresistibly brings to mind the romantic image of a sailing ship. A similar effect might have been achieved by the application of a couple of fake masts to an ordinary portal frame structure. But the true High Tech architect would never resort to such deception. The structure has to be real and there has to be a functional justification for it. In this case, the justification is the low bearing capacity of the subsoil. Of all the possible ways to overcome this problem, the tension structure was chosen, however, not for its economy but for its symbolic power.

Le Corbusier described the house as a machine for living in, but he built houses that were technologically primitive and looked nothing like machines. High Tech buildings do look like machines. The machine is more than a metaphor; it is a source of technology and of imagery. Machines are usually mass-produced, either mobile or portable, and made of synthetic materials such as metal, glass, and plastic. These characteristics have become the reference points of High Tech architecture. The buildings may not be mass-produced, or even assembled from mass-produced components, but they look mass-produced, or at least capable of repetition. They may not be mobile, like cars, or portable, like television sets, but they will usually be made of distinct components and will often appear to hover a few inches above the site as if, one day, they might be dismantled or moved.

Look at Norman Foster's Sainsbury Centre for the Visual Arts (page 58), Michael Hopkins' Brewery in Bury St Edmunds (page 102). These buildings have very different functions – an art gallery and a warehouse – but they are both simple, finely proportioned metal boxes that make no formal concessions to their particular locations. They sit on the ground like pieces of equipment (huge refrigerators, perhaps) airlifted in by giant helicopter. Evidently, their form does not arise from any detailed articulation of the activities housed. But how much is it determined by the technology of their construction, and how much by the wish to give them a machine-like appearance? It is hard to say. Function and representation, engineering and architecture, are delicately balanced.

The mass production problem

An architecture that tries to imitate the methods and products of the manufacturing industry encounters some special problems. Chief among these is the problem of mass production (ill. 1). Cars are made in millions; buildings are usually one-off. It takes many years and very large sums of money to design and develop a car. Many prototypes must be made and tested. If a building is to make use of the same technology, and achieve the same level of sophistication, then there must be a similar level of investment in its design and development. But this is economically out of the question unless identical buildings are to be produced in thousands. There have, of course, been many attempts to industrialize the production of buildings, but no one has yet succeeded in marketing the successful building equivalent of the Model T Ford. It seems that the necessity for constant adaptation to different site conditions and different use requirements means that, in the end, it is usually cheaper to build in bricks and mortar.

Meanwhile, the mass production of certain building components has increased steadily. Windows, doors, curtain wall mullions, raised floors, and suspended ceilings are mass-produced to standard patterns in factories and it is now commonplace for buildings to incorporate whole systems of components. Even buildings that are apparently thoroughly traditional turn out to contain many non-traditional synthetic components and materials, such as asbestos tiles, glass fibre insulation, steel joist hangers, and plastic windows. Building has quietly been industrialized, as it were, behind the architect's back. The technology has changed profoundly, but the architecture has not. High Tech architects want to bring buildings back into line, not by returning to traditional building technology (though this is a possibility seriously proposed by present day neo-classicists), but by creating an architecture that looks mass-produced and machine-like.

There are two obvious answers then, to the mass production problem. The first is to design, develop, manufacture, and market a standard building. This is what Michael Hopkins has tried to do with his Patera buildings (page 104). These are simple but extremely refined, small factory/office buildings. Their details have been developed in collaboration with the manufac-

turer just as if they were vehicles or consumer products. And they have the approved, High Tech, machine-like appearance. They are, however, not cheap and they have failed to find a mass market among the small, go-ahead, image-conscious businesses for which they were designed. It seems that once again bricks and mortar, or their equivalent, have triumphed over the Model T building.

The second answer is to make buildings entirely out of catalogue components. The most famous example of this approach, and one which has had an enormous influence on High Tech, is the Eames house of 1949 in Pacific Palisades (ill. 2). The tradition is carried on in California, mainly by the German architect Helmut Schulitz (pages 140, 144). However, in Britain, the heartland of High Tech, there seems to be a resistance to using mass-produced building products straight and unmodified. Partly, no doubt, this is because of what these British architects consider to be the poor visual quality of these products. A plastic-framed window with fake "Georgian" glazing bars is a highly developed, mass-produced component made entirely of synthetic materials but it is likely to be dismissed with contempt by a Richard Rogers or a Norman Foster. Somehow, the various proprietary components and systems never quite come up to these architects' exacting standards. It is not unusual, therefore, for a High Tech architect to invent and develop his own components and systems and to have them custom-made in small, specialist workshops. The essential thing is not that the component in question, be it glazing mullion, aluminium flashing, steel truss, or pipe sleeve, should be mass-produced, but that it should look right. High Tech has its own flourishing craft tradition.

The other way to solve this aesthetic problem is for the architect to collaborate with product manufacturers in the development of component systems. This often happens in an informal way. A technical representative visits the High Tech architect's office and is promised an order, provided he can alter this profile, conceal that fixing, get rid of that ugly junction. The modifications are made, the deal is done, and the system passes into that select group of products that have the approval of this most demanding group of architects.

Occasionally, in the biggest projects, the collaboration between architect and product designer is formalized. The best example of this is Norman Foster's HongkongBank Headquarters (page 68) in which all the main elements of the building, including the curtain wall, structure cladding, service modules, floors, ceilings, partitions, and furniture, were designed, developed, and tested by architect and manufacturer working together. Norman Foster has

1. Pre-war American aeroplane factory in which Buckminster Fuller proposed to make standard houses.

2. Charles Eames' own house at Pacific Palisades, California, 1949. The catalogue component answer to the mass production problem.

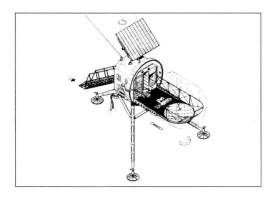

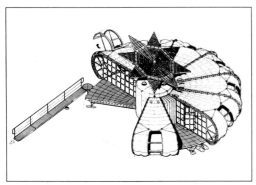

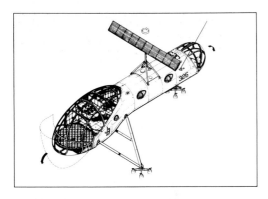

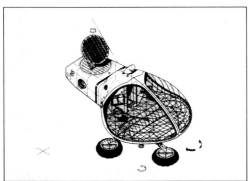

3. Four projects for houses by Jan Kaplicky. The "real" high technology of the aerospace industry brought to bear on the problem of building.

given the process a rather vague title; he calls it simply "design development". A certain percentage of the building budget was allocated to design development from the start, in the same way that a car manufacturer might invest in the development of a new model. The difference is that in building it is the client, not the manufacturer, who pays, which is the reason why design development is so rare.

Foster's great achievement in Hong Kong was that he managed to raise the real quality and sophistication of building technology, instead of merely presenting the image of quality and sophistication. For Jan Kaplicky, however, who once worked for Foster, this is not enough; he feels there is still a very long way to go. Kaplicky is the technological conscience of High Tech. For him there must be no self-deception. He refuses to pretend that merely to use metal, glass, and Neoprene adds up to anything that can be described as "high technology". He wants to bring real high technology, especially the technology of the aerospace industry, to bear on the problem of building (ill. 3).

His is a futuristic architecture, an architecture of "if only": if only structural engineers would abandon their primitive analysis techniques and confront the structural possibilities that modern metallurgy offers; if only someone would develop an airship with sufficient lifting capacity to carry big, prefabricated pieces of buildings; if only some manufacturer would be prepared to make the necessary investment to mass-produce, for example, a complete, integrated bathroom capsule. For the present it remains a dream of a possible future, and Kaplicky's projects (apart from those commissioned, significantly, by NASA) remain theoretical. The building industry, it seems, is not yet ready for real high technology.

Structure and services – The glorification of technology

Exposed structure and exposed services are the two most visible distinguishing features of High Tech architecture, even though not all High Tech architects expose the structure and services of their buildings as a matter of course. In fact this is one of the most important stylistic differences between the two leaders of British High Tech, Norman Foster and Richard Rogers. Rogers loves to drape pipes and ducts all over the facades of his buildings, even if it means that every one has to be separately insulated, protected from the elements, and made accessible for maintenance. There is a functional justification, of course (the "differential life span" argument – see below), but Rogers also frankly admits that the picturesque effect, the play of light and shade, is equally important. Foster, on

the other hand, almost never exposes service ducts, and certainly not on the outside of the building. He prefers to tuck them away behind suspended ceilings, raised floors, and diaphanous screens (see the insides of side walls of the Sainsbury art gallery, page 58 and ill. 4). Rogers loves the bristling, visceral composition; Foster loves the slick, clean skin.

Both, however, are tempted by the expressive power of structure, especially steel structure. Steel is one of the very few building materials that is strong in tension. Given High Tech architecture's tendency to dramatize the technical function of building elements, it is not surprising that steel tension members should be given such prominence. Bear in mind also that the staple diet of the High Tech architect has been the simple industrial shed, a building type that often can hardly be described as architecture at all.

At first the shed was made into architecture by providing it with a shiny metal skin, bright colours and bold graphics. But there is only so much that can be done with such a limited palette, and before too long High Tech architects began to experiment with elaborate decorative tensile structures. Of all the innovative features of that seminal building, Foster and Rogers' Reliance Controls Factory in Swindon of 1967 (ill. 5), it is the external steel cross-bracing (much of it structurally redundant) that has had the most influence on High Tech architecture down the years.

At first it was simply a matter of putting the lattice trusses above the roof rather than below (see, for example, the Patera buildings by Michael Hopkins (page 104) – though these are actually portal frames, not trusses) but this was soon elaborated into a series of variations on the mast and suspension rod theme. All four of the major British High Tech architects have explored the dramatic potential of suspension structures: look at Rogers' Inmos factory (page 26), Foster's Renault warehouse (page 64), Grimshaw's Oxford Ice Rink (page 94), and Hopkins' Schlumberger laboratories (page 108). There are not many good, practical reasons for putting a steel structure on the outside of a building, but plenty of reasons for not doing it. It is exposed to the weather and, therefore, in most cases, needs more frequent maintenance. Painting masts and cables is not an easy or cheap job. And when a roof is suspended from above, it is necessary to puncture the roof membrane at the points of support, creating weak points in the weatherproofing.

Much ingenuity has been applied to solve these problems. At the Oxford Ice Rink, for example, Grimshaw specified expensive but maintenance-free stainless steel for all the tension rods and cleverly minimized the number of points of support by including a heavy internal spine beam. But the technical disadvantages of exposed steel structures remain, and no amount of "justification" (more economical foundations, column-free interiors, increased flexibility) can dispel the conviction that the real reason for their popularity among High Tech architects is that they convert ordinary factory sheds into colourful works of architecture. Black is quite common (Oxford Ice Rink and Schlumberger laboratories) but primary colours are usually preferred for the painted steelwork.

The classics of the type are undoubtedly the Inmos factory in Newport by Richard Rogers (page 26) and its American sister, PA Technology, Princeton (page 32). In these buildings the masts have a double function. They support the roof beams via tension rods, but they also support the mechanical plant over the main circulation spines. This congruence of plan, structure, and services has great conceptual elegance and formal power. These are relatively small buildings, but they have a big architectural presence.

The contribution of the structural engineer to the design of buildings such as these is obviously very important. Two names dominate High Tech engineering: Peter Rice, who designed the PA Technology structure, and Anthony Hunt, who was the structural engineer for no fewer than seven of the buildings illustrated in the main section of this book.

A single-storey building can expose its steel structure to view in all its muscular, metallic glory. But the frame of a multi-storey building must be fireproof. Traditionally, that means either using reinforced concrete or, if the frame is steel, encasing it in concrete. Neither of these is likely to meet with the approval of High Tech architects for whom dry, factory-made, bolted steel is always to be preferred to wet, messy, cast-in-place concrete. At the Centre Pompidou (ill. 6), the problem was solved by a combination of water-cooling for the columns, dry insulation for the trusses, and spray-on fireproofing for the joints. These techniques, however, have not been without their technical and maintenance problems. When Richard Rogers came to design the structure of Lloyd's of London (page 42), water cooling was considered in the early stages, but eventually the decision was made to play safe and opt for a combination of cast-in-place and precast concrete. As a result, the structure, though of very high quality, plays a secondary architectural role.

The structural frame of Foster's HongkongBank Headquarters (page 68), on the other hand, could hardly be more prominent. The floors are not supported on columns in the normal way, but hang from structures very like suspension bridges (known to their designers as "coat hangers"), which in turn are supported by eight massive masts. The original reason, or rather justification, for this unusual structure was the early requirement to retain the old Bank building during construction. This idea was soon abandoned, but the tension structure remained. It offered certain advantages, such as a completely column-free plaza beneath the building; but more important, it had become an essential part of the architecture. The opportunity to use the tensile strength of steel and to give it full expression both inside and outside the building was too good to be missed, even if it meant breaking one of the unwritten laws of High Tech: that materials should always be used with complete honesty. Because the steel had to be fireproofed, by means of a special ceramic fibre insulating blanket, it was then necessary to encase every column, beam, brace, and strut in aluminium in order to preserve the smooth, metallic finish essential to the High Tech aesthetic.

Space and flexibility – The omniplatz

The various elements of a High Tech building – the muscular steel structure, the smooth, impervious skin, the deliberately exposed pipes and air ducts – are often powerfully expressive of their technical function, but the form of the complete building is often remarkably inexpressive of its intended use. The moulding of space, whether to suit particular patterns of use or simply for visual effect, has never been an issue in High Tech architecture. The Lloyd's building (page 42) illustrates this distinction perfectly. Externally it is an extremely complicated object, the elements of which are very clearly articulated and expressive of their functions. There is absolutely no ambiguity: it is perfectly clear which elements are the staircases, which the lifts, which the air ducts. The only possible doubt is about the nature of the internal space being serviced by all these technical contraptions. A glance at the plan reveals the space to be the plainest of rectangles pierced by a central atrium. The purpose of the complicated exterior is precisely to keep the internal space as simple as possible.

The issue of space has been replaced in High Tech architecture by the more technical issue of flexibility. The idea is summed up in the word "omniplatz". What we are providing, say the High Tech architects, is not an enclosure – a room or a hall or a spacial sequence – but a serviced zone. It might be internal or external. The possible uses of this zone are maximized by providing facilities of various kinds – air, heat, light, power, and something to fix partitions to – on a regular grid.

The most obvious example of this is the building that, more than any other, gave the High Tech

4. Sainsbury art gallery (see p. 58). Services hidden away behind diaphanous ceilings and screens.

5. Reliance Controls Factory, Swindon, Wiltshire, by Team 4 (including Richard Rogers and Norman Foster), 1967. First of a long line of simple, elegant factory/office buildings.

6. Centre Pompidou, Paris, by Piano and Rogers, 1977. The columns are water-cooled to improve fire resistance.

7. Interior of the Centre Pompidou. Total commitment to flexibility.

8. Centre Pompidou, showing sections of floor omitted at upper levels.

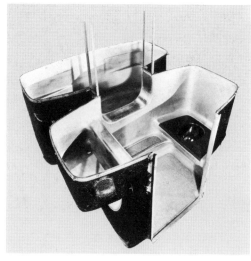

9. Dymaxion bathroom by Buckminster Fuller, 1936. Pioneering the plug-in principle.

10. Service Tower, International Students' Club, London, by Farrell and Grimshaw, 1967. Rival to Reliance Controls Factory (ill. 5) for the title "first British High Tech building".

style its momentum through the 1970s, the Centre Pompidou. As with Lloyd's, there is a contrast between a simple, abstract, rectangular floor plan and a complex, technically expressive exterior. This, however, is a multi-functional building with art galleries, museum, library, theatre, concert hall, and restaurant. Still, the basic elements of the interior, including the massive long-span trusses, remain the same, whatever the function (ill. 7). Space cannot be committed to a single function because the whole design is committed to the idea of flexibility.

Of course there is nothing exclusively High Tech about the omniplatz idea. Most modern office blocks allow a degree of flexibility in the placing and moving of partitions. But the High Tech philosophy takes flexibility a stage further. It introduces the idea that not just partitions but also more permanent elements, such as external walls, roofs, and structural frames should also be demountable. External walls are the common subjects for these exercises in additional flexibility. The elevation, like the plan, becomes an abstract grid that can accommodate a number of different functions: an insulated panel, a door, an opening window, or a metal louvre. When the function of the space changes, the configuration of the external wall can respond accordingly. And because it is an assemblage of tough, dry components, the change can be made in a matter of minutes with simple tools and no mess. That, at least, is the theory. In practice clients very rarely find it necessary to carry out such alterations, but as with so many aspects of High Tech, the abstract concept is at least as important as the practical reality.

It is much less common for structural elements such as frames, floors or roofs to be made demountable in any practical sense. Nevertheless, the idea is often implied in the form of the buildings. The Centre Pompidou, Lloyd's and the HongkongBank are all "incomplete" forms. At the Centre Pompidou, sections of the upper floors are omitted to form open roof terraces (ill. 8); at Lloyd's, the simple hollow rectangle of occupied space is eroded on one side in response to the scale of the surrounding buildings; at the HongkongBank, the three elements of the tower rise to different heights and the upper floors are cut back at the sides, between the main structural masts. All these buildings are open-ended and incomplete, so that floors and other elements of structure could be added or taken away without destroying a perfect composition. Once the principle of general demountability has been established, the building becomes not a single artifact, which will one day wear out or outlive its usefulness, but a collection of artifacts of different types and with different life expectancies. This is the theory behind the High Tech habit of hanging mechanical equipment and services on the outside of the building instead of burying them in the core or basement. The main reinforced concrete frame of a building like Lloyd's is virtually indestructible; it will last forever. The air handling plant, lift motors, wiring and ductwork, on the other hand, might be expected to last 15 or 20 years at the most. It makes sense, therefore, to place them outside the main volume of the building where they can be altered or replaced without interrupting the use of the internal spaces.

The plug-in pod – A practical strategy

There is one High Tech device that combines the various preoccupations with flexibility, demountability, renewability, and mass production. This is the plug-in pod. The sources of this idea are many and various. Buckminster Fuller, the Japanese Metabolists, Archigram, the container revolution, and the development of the offshore oil platform all have made their contributions. The idea of the bathroom pod has been around since at least 1937, when Buckminster Fuller designed the steel prefabricated Dymaxion bathroom (ill. 9). More recently, in 1967, the youthful Nicholas Grimshaw, then in partnership with Terry Farrell, produced a conceptually very advanced cluster of bathroom pods spiralling around a central pipe duct in a circular, glass-clad tower. The tower plugged into the back of nineteenth-century housing converted into a student hostel (ill. 10). Grimshaw has also designed stainless steel toilet modules, suitable for mass production, and installed prototypes in his economical industrial buildings (ill. 11).

For Japanese Metabolists like Kisho Kurokawa the plug-in pod was not just a service module, it was a personal dwelling capsule. The Nagakin Capsule Tower of 1972 (ill. 14) is a building composed almost entirely of plug-in pods, and no doubt owes a great deal to Peter Cook's Plug-in City project of 1964 (ill. 13) – a whole city of plug-in pods.

But the best examples are again those two High Tech tours de force, the Lloyd's building and the HongkongBank. It is the Lloyd's building that gives the idea clearest expression. 33 shiny, stainless steel-clad boxes with round windows are stacked up in concrete-framed towers like shoe boxes on racks (ill. 12). The boxes, or pods, contain the toilets, perhaps the most architecturally expressive toilets ever built. It appears that the concrete frames were built first and the pods slotted in subsequently. Visually, the clear implication is that the pods can be unplugged and replaced by new pods when they wear out, or perhaps that they might be moved to another

11. Plug-in toilet module for advance factory units at Warrington, Cheshire, by Nicholas Grimshaw, 1978.

12. Toilet module being hoisted into place on the Lloyd's building (see p. 42).

13. Plug-in City project by Peter Cook and Archigram, 1964.

14. Nagakin Capsule Tower, Tokyo, by Kisho Kurokawa, 1972. Plug-in pods as living capsules.

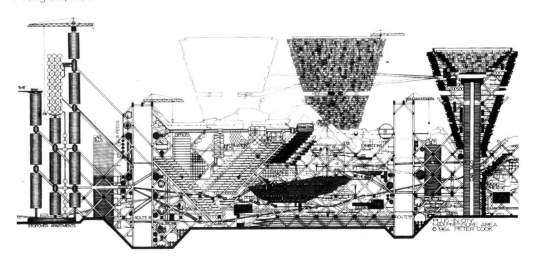

15. Interior of service module in the HongkongBank (see p. 68). Toilet area in the foreground, air handling plant beyond.

16. Modern Art Glass factory at Thamesmead, near London, by Norman Foster, 1973. An only slightly more elegant version of the metal sheds that are common on industrial estates all over Britain.

17. Rogers House, Wimbledon, London, by Richard and Su Rogers, 1979.

location in response to some alteration in the use of the building. But in fact the two elements, frame and pods, were assembled in parallel, floor by floor, and it would be extremely difficult to separate them. As usual with High Tech, the idea and its visual expression are as important as the practicality.

The equivalent pods at the HongkongBank are slightly different, both in function and expression (ill. 15). As at Lloyd's, they contain the toilets, but they also contain the localized air handling plant. At Lloyd's the possibility of the building owner ever wishing to replace the toilet pods is very remote. Toilets do not, after all, wear out very quickly. Air handling plants do wear out quickly, and it therefore makes more sense for the Hong Kong pods to be unpluggable. In fact, however, they too are permanently fixed in place, and the stacks of pods have been clad in a continuous aluminium skin so they do not even look unpluggable.

But renewability is only one of the reasons for the use of plug-in pods. The main reason, and an eminently practical one, is that it enables complicated and highly finished parts of the building to be made on a production line and shipped to the site complete, fully fitted out, and tested. This offers three important advantages. First, it speeds up work on site, since the building and fitting out of the pods can proceed in parallel with the construction of the main frame of the building. Second, it improves the quality of the product, which is being made in clean, controlled workshop conditions, and not in the chaotic and dirty environment of the building site. Third, since mechanical plant, pipework and ductwork are being installed at ground level on a production line with access all round, it can be arranged much more compactly. (This, of course, might turn out to be a disadvantage if the plant has to be replaced at a later date, in position in the building.)

All these are real, practical advantages. There is one more possible advantage, but here again we are in the realms of theory rather than practicality. One might assume that all the pods for one building, and possibly the pods for several buildings, would be identical and therefore suitable for mass production. This would be the High Tech ideal: to make buildings, or at least substantial parts of buildings, the way cars are made. In practice, however, this seems to be almost impossible to achieve. Buildings are just too big, too complicated, and too specialized. There are 139 service pods in the Hongkong-Bank and no two are identical.

The typology of High Tech

The whole idea of a building typology based on function or use seems irrelevant when the aim is to make buildings flexible enough to adapt to almost any use. In practice, however, High Tech is commonly associated with a rather narrow range of building types.

The typical High Tech building is a factory. In fact, so pervasive has been the influence of the High Tech style on factory design that we can now almost say that the typical factory is High Tech. The old factory archetype – a brick-clad building with a saw-tooth northlight roof and a tall chimney – has been replaced by the shiny metal-clad shed painted a bright colour and decorated with bold graphics. High Tech, of a more or less diluted kind, has become a sort of vernacular for factory building. Norman Foster's Modern Art Glass factory at Thamesmead (ill. 16) or Nicholas Grimshaw's Herman Miller warehouse at Chippenham (page 88) are only slightly more elegant versions of the metal shed that is common on industrial and research parks all over Britain.

The factory type, defined as a long span structure with a simple skin enclosing an undifferentiated space, has been adapted in recent years to house other functions. Supermarkets, leisure centres and even art galleries are likely, these days, to resemble factories in their basic form. They have therefore become suitable cases for the High Tech treatment. Look, for example, at the Sainsbury supermarket in Canterbury by Ahrends, Burton and Koralek (page 114); the Link Centre in Swindon by Thamesdown Borough Council (page 130); and Foster's Sainsbury Centre for the Visual Arts at the University of East Anglia (page 58). Modern offices, too, especially those sited in so-called "science parks", are likely to be housed in High Tech sheds. Indeed, as modern industry becomes cleaner and quieter, the distinction between office and factory becomes increasingly blurred. The factory has taken over from the house as the characteristic modern building type.

It is in housing that the influence of High Tech has been weakest. Here we have to make a distinction between house and housing. There are plenty of examples of individual houses that are thoroughgoing exercises in the High Tech style. It may be significant, however, that a high proportion of these are occupied either by their designers or by relatives of their designers: the Hopkins House (page 100), the Schulitz House (page 140), the Rogers House (ill. 17), the Benthem and Crouwel House (page 148) and so on. High Tech of the purest kind creates a hard, metallic, austere environment that few people would describe as domestic. The very few examples of High Tech mass housing, such as Foster's housing at Milton Keynes (ill. 18), have not been successful. When High Tech architects tackle housing, they commonly resort to traditional building methods and materials.

If High Tech is biased toward certain building types, it is also biased toward certain types of client. It is perhaps not surprising, given High Tech architects' enthusiasm for industrial technology, that their clients should commonly be industrial and business corporations. By transforming the imagery of manufacturing industry into an architectural style, High Tech reinforces industrial capitalism's claim to be working for the general good. It is the willing servant of industrial society, ready to receive instructions from those in power and carry out its task conscientiously. When it adopts a critical stance it is usually on a technological and institutional rather than a political level.

The Centre Pompidou is designed to break down the traditional boundaries between different forms of high culture and make them accessible to a wider public. To that extent it is a critical statement. It claims to be neutral and value free, a multi-purpose tool to be used and enjoyed in many different ways. But it is also an obvious celebration of industrial technology and therefore, despite itself, transmits its own clear cultural message. Some of High Tech's critics – the promoters of "community architecture", participatory design, and alternative technology – are quick to point out that advanced technology has its dark side. For them, High Tech architecture is a glorification not of technology itself, but of "the military/industrial complex".

Revolution versus continuity – High Tech and the city

High Tech's natural affinity with the factory as a building type has important implications for its relationship with the city. The three biggest and most important High Tech buildings – the Centre Pompidou, Lloyd's and the HongkongBank (ills. 19, 20, 21) – are city buildings, and their architects would certainly claim that an urban context had a profound effect on their design. Nevertheless, it is true to say that urbanistic concerns, like the manipulation of space, are not a major element in the High Tech philosophy. For the High Tech architect, space is an abstract entity that is devoid of specific qualities until it is inhabited and adapted by its users. But for the urbanist, or contextualist, space is necessarily specific because it is defined by its relationship to the context of the city.

Take, for example, the Lloyd's building. It occupies an irregular site bordered by streets and alleyways of different scales with very different spacial qualities and patterns of use. The building responds to these irregularities only in a limited way. The boxlike form of the main volume steps down on one side to acknowledge the difference in scale of the surrounding buildings, and the service towers are arranged to fit

18. Housing at Milton Keynes, Buckinghamshire, by Norman Foster. Unsuccessful attempt to apply High Tech to mass housing.

21. HongkongBank in context.

19. Centre Pompidou. Urban context is not an overriding concern of High Tech architects.

20. The Lloyd's building seen through Tower Bridge. A picturesque profile disguising a diagrammatic plan.

13

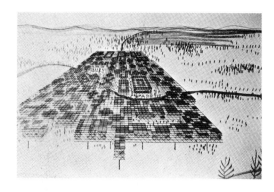

22. "Ville Spatiale" project by Yona Friedman, 1959. Fixed infrastructure with movable secondary elements.

23. Iron bridge at Coalbrookdale, Shropshire, 1779. First High Tech structure.

24. Palm House at Kew Gardens, London, by Decimus Burton, 1848. Victorian glass and metal architecture is an enduring influence on British architects.

25. St Pancras Station, London, 1865.

26. Galerie des Machines by Dutert and Contamin, at the Paris Exhibition of 1889.

27. The Crystal Palace, London, by Joseph Paxton, 1851. The prefabricated metal and glass building par excellence, dismantled and relocated in 1854.

into the leftover corners of the site. But these are adaptations of a perfect diagram, and it is the diagram that takes precedence. It is as if the city were not allowing the building to be what it wants to be. Freestanding buildings on green field sites (the Inmos factory, for example, page 26), which do not have to adapt to their context, are more characteristic of the High Tech style.

Foster's Willis, Faber and Dumas office building in Ipswich (page 56) is another case in point. It fits its irregular site perfectly, its all-glass, serpentine external wall conforming precisely to the site boundary. Claims have been made for it as a contextual building because it reflects (literally) the older buildings that surround it. The reflective serpentine wall, however, is just another way to adapt a centralized, inward-looking, diagrammatic, spacially uniform and typically High Tech plan. Of course most building plans can be reduced to diagrams, which is not in itself anti-urban. But it is a question of priorities. One only has to look, for example, at the recent work of James Stirling to see the very different architecture that results when context is given priority over diagram.

There is another reason why urbanism is not a major element of the High Tech philosophy, and that is its lack of relationship with the past. High Tech is a forward-looking, optimistic architecture that believes in progress through industrial technology. It believes in invention rather than tradition, in temporary arrangements rather than permanent institutions, and in the ability to control the environment rather than adapting to it. If the city is the embodiment of tradition, permanence, continuity, and history then High Tech is an anti-urban style. High Tech buildings imply a revolutionary, rather than a traditional, view of the city. If a complete High Tech city were ever to be built it would be an abstract, fully serviced matrix or megastructure, flexible and demountable, like the utopian urban visions of the 1960s: Peter Cook's Plug-in City (ill. 13), Yona Friedman's "Ville Spatiale" (ill. 22), or the indeterminate city structures envisaged by the Japanese Metabolists. In these theoretical projects, as in their built High Tech counterparts, structure, access, services, and equipment are more important than space and place, whether internal or external, private or public.

From ironbridge to the Challenger space craft – A short history of High Tech

Where did High Tech architecture come from? There are two useful historical perspectives of long range and short range, of 200 years and 20 years. For the long-range perspective we have to go back to 1779 and the construction of the

14

first cast iron bridge over the River Severn at Coalbrookdale (ill. 23). It is an all-metal prefabricated structure, completely honest in its use of materials and structural forms, but designed as much for elegance as for practicality. In the long term, this must be the favourite candidate for the title "first High Tech structure".

This may seem like far too remote a source for an architectural style born in the 1960s, but the bridge is still standing and we should not underestimate the influence of eighteenth- and nineteenth-century engineering structures on British architects. Decimus Burton's Palm House at Kew Gardens of 1848 (ill. 24), the long-span iron, steel and glass roofs over the great railway termini built throughout the second half of the nineteenth century (ill. 25), Eiffel's tower and Contamin and Dutert's Galerie des Machines built for the Paris Exhibition of 1889 (ill. 26), and of course Paxton's legendary Crystal Palace built for the Great Exhibition of 1851 (ill. 27) — structures such as these are enduring influences on today's High Tech architects. They represent an alternative mode of building, based on industrial technology rather than architectural tradition. High Tech architecture shares their confidence and optimism and also, to a large extent, their relatively primitive technology.

Throughout the first half of the twentieth century it was to remain an alternative rather than a mainstream mode of building. The characteristic material of Modern-movement mainstream is reinforced concrete, exactly the sort of wet, in situ material that High Tech architects prefer to avoid. Mies van der Rohe is, of course, the exception, but building technology was never his primary concern. The most famous of all Mies construction details — the decorative steel pilasters on the Seagram building (ill. 28) — has a dishonesty that most true High Tech architects would deplore. Nevertheless certain habits, the use of external structure, for example, can be traced back to Mies.

Except in structures that we think of as "pure engineering", the alternative Modernism was kept alive mainly in theoretical projects, most notably those of the Italian Futurists and the Russian Constructivists. The perspective sketches of Sant' Elia's Citta Nuova (ill. 29), exhibited in 1914, are among the earliest depictions of an architecture that glorifies the technology of concrete, steel, and glass, and which gives dramatic external expression of lift towers, girder bridges, and elevated walkways. The similarities to the more sculpturesque examples of the High Tech style, especially the work of Richard Rogers, are striking. "We no longer believe in the monumental, the heavy and static, and have enriched our sensibilities with a taste for lightness, transience and practicality," wrote Sant' Elia in the catalogue to the Citta Nuova

28. Seagram Building, New York, by Mies van der Rohe, 1958. High Tech owes an obvious debt to Mies but has a more rigorous attitude to structural honesty.

29. Study from the Citta Nuova by Sant' Elia, 1913. Dynamic expression of movement and structure.

30. One of Iakov Chernikhov's Constructivist fantasies of the 1930s. An alternative modernism kept alive in theoretical projects.

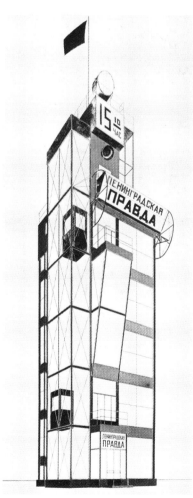

31. Alexander Vesnin's 1923 project for the Pravda building in Moscow. Proto-High Tech, complete with techno-romantic add-ons: a searchlight where one would now expect a satellite dish.

32. Dutch Constructivism. Van Nelle Tobacco Factory, Rotterdam, 1930, by Brinkman and van der Vlugt with Mart Stam.

34. Maison du Peuple, Clichy, by Beaudouin and Lods with the French High Tech pioneer, Jean Prouvé, 1939.

33. Maison de Verre, Paris, by Pierre Chareau and Bernard Bijvoet, 1932. An acknowledged influence on Richard Rogers.

35. Dymaxion House project, 1927, by Buckminster Fuller, American guru of High Tech.

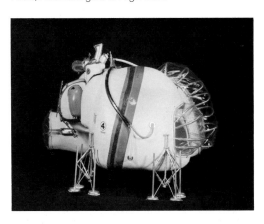

36. Living Pod project by David Greene of Archigram, 1965. A landing module for the planet Earth.

exhibition. "We must invent and rebuild ex novo our modern city like an immense and tumultuous shipyard, active, mobile and everywhere dynamic, and the modern building like a gigantic machine. Lifts must not longer hide away like solitary worms in the stairwells... but must swarm up the facades like serpents of glass and iron."[3] The Centre Pompidou and the Lloyd's building would be quite at home in the Citta Nuova.

With the Russian Constructivists we come even closer to the precise sensibilities of High Tech. Look, for example, at Iakov Chernikhov's "Fantasies" (ill. 30), the Constructivist equivalent of Sant' Elia's visionary drawings; or at Alexander Vesnin's project for the Pravda building in Moscow of 1923 (ill. 31). This bristles with proto-High Tech motifs, such as diagonal steel cross-bracing, lifts in glass shafts and even what appears to be a satellite dish on the roof (in fact it is a searchlight). We can even begin, at this point, to trace direct and acknowledged influences on High Tech. In Western Europe, the influence of Constructivism was felt most strongly in the Netherlands and is most visible in the work of Mart Stam (ill. 32, who collaborated with El Lissitsky, the chief propagandist of Constructivism) and Johannes Duiker. Duiker's partner, Bernard Bijvoet, was to collaborate with Pierre Chareau in the design of the Maison de Verre in Paris, completed in 1932 (ill. 33). This building is a curious assemblage of mass-produced, machine-like components with a flexible plan and an external wall made entirely of glass lenses. In 1959 Richard Rogers visited the Maison de Verre and he now acknowledges it as the building that has had the most influence on his architecture.

While Chareau and Bijvoet were designing the Maison de Verre, Jean Prouvé was developing the first system of replaceable wall components for lightweight metal houses. Prouvé was to continue to develop his own, peculiarly French, metal and glass architecture right up to the 1970s (ill. 34). The extent of his influence on British High Tech can be gauged by Norman Foster's remark when he invited Prouvé to visit his office: "We would never have done all this without you."

Meanwhile, on the other side of the Atlantic, Buckminster Fuller was proposing an even more thoroughgoing application of advanced technology in his Dymaxion House project of 1927 (ill. 35), a hexagonal structure of lightweight metal and plastic suspended from a core of mechanical services. If anyone deserves the title "father of High Tech" it is Fuller. His comprehensive and knowledgeable use of materials and technology borrowed from other industries (the Dymaxion House proposed an adaptation of techniques used in aircraft construction at that time), his insistence on a global view of building performance (architects, he said, should know not just how big their buildings were, or how much they cost but also how much they weighed), and his refusal to have anything to do with the conventions of traditional, academic architecture – these have all been built solidly into the ideological structure of High Tech.

It was Reyner Banham, in the closing pages of *Theory and Design in the First Machine Age*,[4] who first introduced Fuller to British architects as a possible model for the future development of modern architecture. This was in 1960 and coincided with an outpouring of formally and technologically inventive projects from students and teachers at London schools of architecture, especially the Regent Street Polytechnic and the Architectural Association. The group called Archigram (Peter Cook, Warren Chalk, David Greene, Denis Crompton, Ron Herron and Mike Webb) began to publish and exhibit spectacular theoretical projects that clearly displayed many of the features of the High Tech architecture of the 1970s and 1980s: the indeterminate forms, the mass-produced, expendable, plug-in components, the use of technologies from the emerging aerospace industry (ills. 36, 37) and, above all, the idea that architects had a duty to increase personal, environmental choice. Architectural historian Robin Middleton has remarked that in the 1960s Archigram did for architecture what the Beatles did for music.

Richard Rogers, Nicholas Grimshaw, and Michael Hopkins were all students at the AA. Of the big four High Tech architects, only Norman Foster, who studied at Liverpool school of architecture, was not directly exposed to the influence of the AA in the early 1960s. There is no doubt that projects such as Michael Webb's "bowellist" Furniture Manufacturer's Association Headquarters, a student project of 1958 (ill. 38), Cedric Price's Fun Palace of 1963 (ill. 39), Peter Cook's Plug-in City of 1964 (ill. 13), and Ron Herron's Walking City of the same year (ill. 40) were well known to Rogers, Foster and co. They were, after all, well known much further afield, largely due to the publicizing efforts of Reyner Banham. The capsule buildings of the Japanese Metabolists (ill. 14), for example, surely owe a debt to Cook's Plug-in City. But we must not make the mistake of assuming that High Tech is simply built Archigram. There were other, and possibly more important, contemporary influences, both British and American.

Of the British influences, Alison and Peter Smithson and James Stirling are the most important. All were teachers at the Architectural Association at the relevant time. The Smithsons' Hunstanton School (ill. 41), designed in 1949 and sometimes described as "Miesian brutalist", was one of the very few British postwar buildings

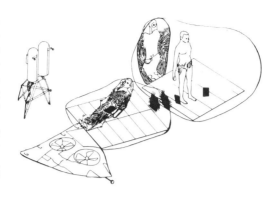

37. Suitaloon: Cushicle, project by Mike Webb of Archigram, 1968. Borrowing the technology and imagery of the emerging aerospace industry.

41. Interior, Hunstanton School, Norfolk, by Alison and Peter Smithson, 1954. Materials displayed with complete honesty.

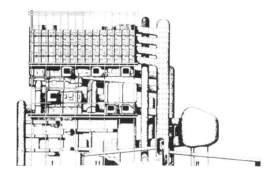

38. 1958 student project by Mike Webb, member of Archigram and inventor of "Bowellism".

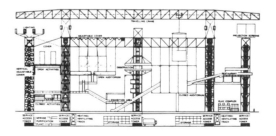

39. Fun Palace project by Cedric Price, 1963. Extreme version of the flexible "omniplatz".

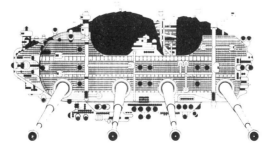

40. Walking City project by Ron Herron of the Archigram group, 1964. Architecture as science fiction.

42. Engineering Building at Leicester University by Stirling and Gowan, 1963. Constructivism and nineteenth-century engineering combined.

43. History Faculty Library at Cambridge University by James Stirling, 1964. Steel trusses over the reading room, visible from within the building.

44. History Faculty Library. Air extract units slung between the trusses are painted in bright colours – a typical High Tech gesture.

45. Richards Memorial Laboratories, Philadelphia, by Louis Kahn, 1961. Kahn's concept of "served" and "servant" spaces became one of the principles of High Tech planning.

46. Charles Eames' own house, at Pacific Palisades, California, 1949.

to be accorded any respect by the 1950s avant garde. It had a curiously formal, Palladian plan, but what made it revolutionary at the time was the way it displayed with complete honesty its materials – steel frame, brick infill, precast concrete floors, exposed electrical conduit and pipework, and a proprietary steel water tank raised on a freestanding steel frame like a campanile. James Stirling's Engineering Building at Leicester University, designed in partnership with James Gowan in 1959 and completed in 1963 (ill. 42) is another historical marker in the development of British Modernism. A powerful composition in red tile-clad concrete and patent glazing, it combined constructivism, nineteenth-century engineering, and the colours and textures of red-brick city of Leicester in such an utterly convincing way that it made James Stirling's international reputation almost overnight.

Both of these buildings can be seen, with hindsight, to contain the seeds of High Tech and both were, without question, powerful influences during High Tech's "student years". The influence of Stirling, in particular, must be emphasized. If it were not for his subsequent metamorphosis into Britain's leading Post-Modernist, and therefore at the opposite stylistic pole from High Tech, we might now be describing his 1964 History Faculty Library at Cambridge University as the first British High Tech building. It has so many of the High Tech motifs: a glass skin, a freestanding lift and service tower, a prominent roof-mounted maintenance crane, huge lattice trusses over the reading room (ill. 43) and, most telling, three air extract units slung between the trusses, clearly visible from below and painted in primary colours (ill. 44).

Rogers, Foster and Stirling all came together for a brief period in 1962 at Yale University where Rogers and Foster were postgraduate students, collaborating for the first time, and Stirling was a visiting critic. The influence of American architects such as Paul Rudolph (then chairman of the architecture school at Yale) and Louis Kahn are detectable in some of the later High Tech buildings. Kahn's concept of "served" and "servant" spaces is especially important: compare the satellite servant towers of Rogers' Lloyd's building with the brick-clad service towers of Kahn's Richards Medical Research Building in Philadelphia, of 1961 (ill. 45). But the strongest American influence was Californian – the simple, flexible, lightweight steel and glass houses of Charles Eames (ill. 46), Craig Ellwood, and Raphael Soriano (ill. 47). These were illustrated in a 1962 book by Esther McCoy called *Modern California Houses* (republished in 1978 as *Case Study Houses: 1945–1962*), which was to be a source of inspiration for 18

Rogers and Foster when they returned to England and set up in practice together under the name Team 4.

Team 4's first important building, a house at Creek Vean in Cornwall (ill. 48), could not remotely be described as High Tech. Concrete blockwork was its main material and its main influence was not Archigram or Eames but Frank Lloyd Wright. The only advanced technical feature was the Neoprene used to seal the sloping glazing. (The Neoprene gasket was to become one of the distinguishing marks of High Tech in its formative years.)

In the short-range, 20-year perspective of the history of High Tech, the title "first British High Tech building" must go to the simple, single-storey Reliance Controls Electronics Factory of 1967 at Swindon (ill. 5). Ironically this was the last building on which Rogers and Foster collaborated. It was Miesian in conception and owed a lot to the much larger Cummins Engine Company factory at Darlington (ill. 49), designed by the American firm of Kevin Roche, John Dinkeloo and Associates and completed in 1965. It had a simple rectangular plan, a flat roof, and a freestanding water tower copied from the Smithsons' Hunstanton School. It would have been quite unremarkable were it not for the exposed steel structure (painted white), the flexible and extendable multi-purpose plan, and the way that it was rapidly assembled from dry, off-the-shelf components. This was the first of a long line of simple, elegant factory/office buildings designed by High Tech architects for High Tech (in the industrial sense) clients. It was instantly acclaimed by critics, won the *Financial Times* award for the most outstanding industrial building of 1967, and gave its designers the confidence to develop their new style with renewed energy.

A close rival for the title "first British High Tech building" is the glass-clad spiral of plastic bathroom pods designed in 1967 by Nicholas Grimshaw to plug into the rear of a Victorian house being converted into a student hostel by his then partner Terry Farrell (ill. 10). In Reliance Controls, the mechanical services had been hidden in a floor duct, so it was Grimshaw who first realized the plug-in servant tower concept that was to become a prominent High Tech motif in subsequent years.

The High Tech repertoire was now complete and for the next ten years each element was developed with ever-increasing confidence in successive buildings and projects by Rogers, Grimshaw, Foster and Michael Hopkins, who joined Foster's office in 1969. There was the slick glass and Neoprene skin of Foster's Amenity Centre for the Fred Olsen shipping line in the London Docks (ill. 50), the severely minimal single-storey office building for IBM at Cosham,

47. Curtis House, Bel Air, California, by Raphael Soriano. Typical of the houses illustrated in Esther McCoy's book *Modern California Houses* which was an early source of inspiration for Rogers and Foster.

48. House at Creek Vean in Cornwall by Team 4, 1966. Only the Neoprene gaskets in the patent glazing can be described as High Tech.

49. Cummins Engine Company factory at Darlington by Kevin Roche, John Dinkeloo and Associates, 1963. Mies plus Neoprene gaskets: a strong influence on Team 4's Reliance Controls Factory.

50. Detail of Norman Foster's amenity building for the Fred Olsen shipping line in the London Docks, 1971. A typical Foster sleek skin of glass and Neoprene.

51. IBM office building at Cosham, Hampshire, by Norman Foster with Michael Hopkins, 1971.

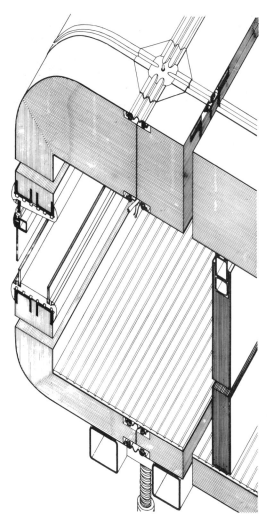

52. Richard Rogers' version of the Neoprene gasket detail. Project for a zip-up autonomous house, 1968.

53. Italian High Tech. Italian Pavilion for Expo '70, Osaka, by Renzo Piano with Tommaso and Gilberto Valle.

54. The Centre Pompidou, Paris, by Piano and Rogers, completed 1977. High Tech enters the public consciousness.

55. Centre Pompidou from the south by night. The Archigram dream realized.

designed by Foster and Hopkins in 1971 (ill. 51), Farrell and Grimshaw's factories for Herman Miller, and a series of vehicle-like buildings and projects by Rogers, with highly insulated, zip-up skins and round-cornered windows fixed, once again, with Neoprene gaskets (ill. 52).

In 1970 Rogers entered into partnership with Renzo Piano, who had been developing his own, highly sophisticated Italian version of High Tech in his office in Genoa (ill. 53). In 1971 the new partnership entered and won the international competition for the design of a new national art and culture centre on the Plateau Beaubourg in Paris. With the Centre Pompidou, High Tech came of age (ills. 54, 55). Pompidou had everything: flexible plan, exposed structure, plug-in services, and the glorification of machine technology. When it was completed in 1977, the image of High Tech suddenly came into focus, entered the public consciousness, and became an internationally influential style. Some of the best examples of that style, mainly from the decade after Pompidou, are illustrated in this book.

So the 20-year story of High Tech has a beginning, the Reliance Controls Factory, a middle, the Centre Pompidou and, just possibly, an end in the two masterpieces completed in 1986, the HongkongBank Headquarters by Norman Foster and Lloyd's of London by Richard Rogers. For there are signs that High Tech is running out of steam. The latest Rogers and Foster projects demonstrate a diminishing interest in technology and a new concern for the less tangible aspects of the complex relationships between people and spaces, and between buildings and cities.

Foster's design for a Médiathèque in the centre of Nîmes (ill. 56), opposite the Roman Temple known as the Maison Carrée, proposes a very un-High Tech palette of materials: concrete, bronze and local stone. On an early published sketch there appears the following note: "No diagonals in structure – must not look 'industrial'." And Foster's abortive scheme for the new headquarters for BBC Radio in London (ill. 57) is curiously subdued – a humble exercise in urban contextualism rather than a glorification of technology. Rogers, too, seems to have discovered the existing city as an architectural theme. When asked to provide a theoretical project for the 1986 Foster, Rogers, Stirling exhibition at the Royal Academy, he presented a scheme for the revitalization of London's South Bank. The scheme included a bombastic and highly technological new bridge across the Thames (ill. 58), but its main thrust was an almost Baroque realignment of vistas and reinforcement of public spaces.

But perhaps the most important change has been in the technological, rather than the architectural, climate. Technology has moved on and once again left architecture behind. There may be an architectural equivalent of the jet aeroplane or the lunar module, but there is no architectural equivalent of the silicon chip. The aerospace industry has always been the happy image-hunting ground of the High Tech architect but it no longer holds the fascination and promise that it did in the late 1960s and early 1970s. Architectural scholiasts of the future, wishing to pin down the precise date of the death of the High Tech style, might well choose January 28th 1986, the day the Challenger space craft blew up in front of the watching millions. The cause of the tragedy, we now know, was the failure of a Neoprene gasket.

58. Project by Richard Rogers for a new bridge over the Thames. A futuristic composition, but only part of a larger plan for the revitalization of the South Bank.

Notes

1 See Buchanan, P. "A Nostalgic Utopia", *Architects Journal,* 4 Sept. 1985, pp. 60–69.
2 See Pugin, A. W. N. *The True Principles of Pointed or Christian Architecture,* London, 1841, p. 1; quoted in: Davey, P. "Pugin Pointed the Way", *Architectural Review,* May 1984, pp. 20–23.
3 Quoted in: Appleyard, B. *Richard Rogers,* Faber and Faber, London, 1986, p. 179 f.
4 Banham, R. *Theory and Design in the First Machine Age,* Architectural Press, London, 1960, pp. 325–329.

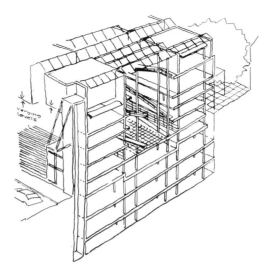

56. Sketch by Norman Foster for the Médiathèque at Nîmes. The industrial image is now suppressed.

57. Project by Norman Foster for a new BBC Broadcasting Centre in London. A curiously subdued building, hypersensitive to its urban context.

**Fleetguard Manufacturing and Distribution Centre,
Quimper, France
Architects: Richard Rogers Partnership
Completed 1981**

The site is next to a main road in a newly designated industrial zone within a few kilometres of the town of Quimper in Brittany. There are magnificent views across the country towards Quimper and the south Brittany coast.

Fleetguard is a subsidiary of the Cummins Engine Company based in Columbus, Indiana, and specializes in manufacturing heavy-duty engine filters. The new plant at Quimper includes production lines for air, fuel, and oil filters, storage facilities, and an administrative headquarters. The total floor area is 95,000 sq.ft./8,750 m^2, with potential for expansion up to 430,000 sq.ft./40,000 m^2 over fifteen years.

The programme called for a building of the highest architectural quality, which would firmly establish the company in mainland Europe. It had to be a highly adaptable building, capable of responding to changing needs and functions and able to expand either within the phasing strategy or in smaller increments to accommodate a more gradual but continuous expansion. The project was financed jointly by Fleetguard and the town of Quimper, which was anxious to provide new industry in an area of high unemployment.

The design aims to minimize the intrusion into the landscape by mounding the surplus excavated soil into a carefully controlled landscape scheme, relegating access roads to the perimeter of the site and segregating industrial from personnel traffic. The stairwell, enclosed in glass, is the focal point of the plan, linking the production and administrative areas.

The use of a dynamic suspension structure reduces the roof span, the structural depth, and the overall mass of the building. At the same time there are economies in enclosed volume, the amount of steel used, energy consumption and surface area. The external structure also frees the interior of the roof for flexible services distribution, unhindered by the beam depth of a conventional frame of similar span. It has the further advantage that the structural connections necessary for extending the building can be made without removing existing cladding and disrupting the use of the building.

The structure consists of elements that require very little fabrication and can be simply joined. Site connections are either bolted or pinned. Major structural connections that have to be made in the air are pinned. Total steel weight is 47 kg per square metre, about 17% less than for conventional structures of comparable bay size.

The cladding is clearly articulated from the structural frame to facilitate bay-by-bay expansion without disrupting the activities within. It is also separated from the roof zone by a continuous band of high-level glazing that brings natural light into all parts of the building.

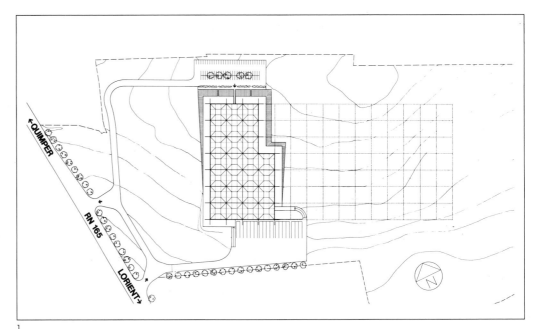

1

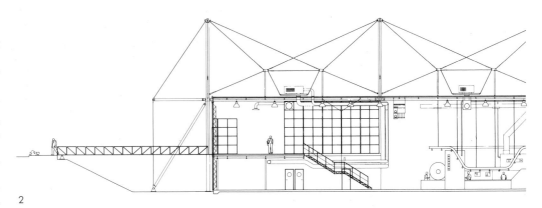

2

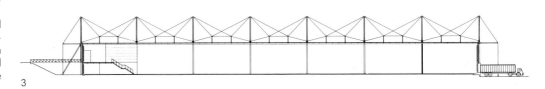

3

1. Site plan.

2. Section showing the entrance bridge on the employee side of the building.

3. North-south section.

4
5
6

4. The suspension structure reduces the bulk of the building in the landscape while signalling its presence in bright red.

5. Mast detail: an assemblage of simple, repetitive elements.

6. The external structure gives scale and proportion to an otherwise featureless building mass.

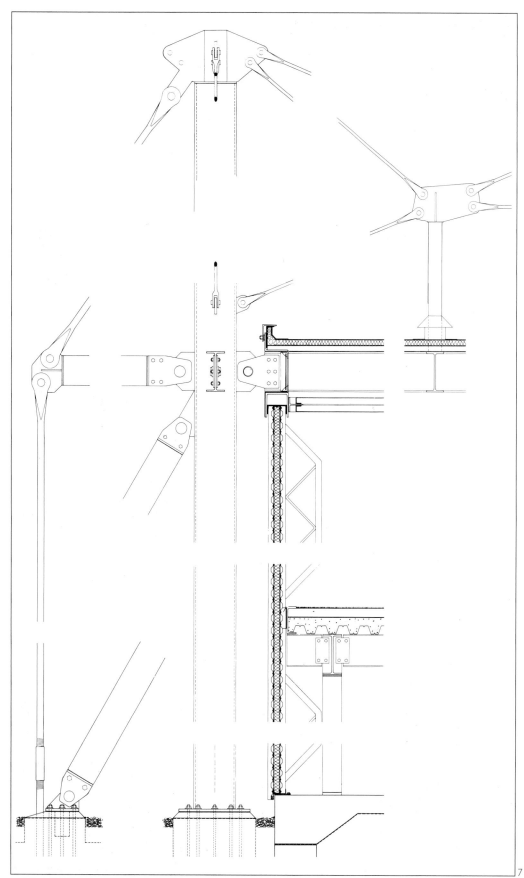

7

8

7. Detail section. A continuous strip of high-level glazing separates roof from vertical support structure.

8. Lateral restraint is by external tubular-steel push/pull braces.

9. Model of one structural bay.

10. The external structure reduces the depth of roof beams and frees the distribution of high level services.

11. Internal glazed partitions between administrative and production spaces.

12. Reception area on the north side of the building.

13. Staircase linking offices and factory: ductwork as decoration.

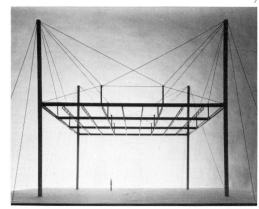

9

10

12

11

13

25

**Inmos Microprocessor Factory, Newport,
South Wales
Architects: Richard Rogers Partnership
Completed 1982**

The programme was for office and ancillary space as well as facilities for microchip wafer production. Speed of design and construction were critical factors. A further constraint on the design was the exceptionally high quality of environmental control required by the microchip production process which is extremely sensitive to dust. Air in the production area had to be absolutely clean to cut down the failure rate of wafer production.

The architects added a series of additional requirements: that the design be able to respond to changes in the programme as it evolved during construction; that the building be both a high performance precision production machine and a friendly and stimulating environment for employees; that the design allow for maximum potential growth and change in order to meet the needs of a new and fast-evolving industry; and that the design and construction principles suit the client's fast building programme.

The building design evolved as a single-storey steel structure conceived as a kit of prefabricated parts to allow the building to be erected rapidly, bay by bay. The basic concept of phase one is a central circulation and service spine with internal wings for specialized activities. The spine, 23'/7.2 m wide and 348'/106 m long, acts as an internal street or informal promenade. It is wide enough to contain vending machines, public telephones, seating, meeting places, planted areas, and waiting areas for the offices. It provides total visual security control and is intended to link up with other future phases of building on the site.

Offices and restaurants are on the south side of the spine and the clean room production area to the north. The main air supply equipment is grouped in localized modules to minimize duct runs above the spine. Ducts are taken across the roof to the point of use. Production wastes are collected in floor trenches and production supply services are distributed on service walls within the production zone. The building is infinitely extendable along the spine. More of the 42' x 118'/13 m x 36 m bays can be added as required, with additional easy access service modules.

The tubular-steel assisted span structure is supported by tension rods from the spine towers. The structural system provides column-free spaces for maximum planning flexibility. The roof is 20'/6 m span steel decking with thermal insulation and a five-layer roof membrane.

The external walls are based on a system of standardized mullions that accept any type of infill: single glazing, double glazing, translucent or opaque panels. This allows the client to alter wall performances and finishes as wished. The initial design proposed double glazing on the office areas and solid insulated sandwich panels for the production areas.

1. Site plan showing proposed extension to twenty bays.

2. Roof plan of phase one.

3. Detail, cross section showing the central spine, with air treatment plant above.

4. Detail, longitudinal section through laboratory showing roof-mounted plant in elevation.

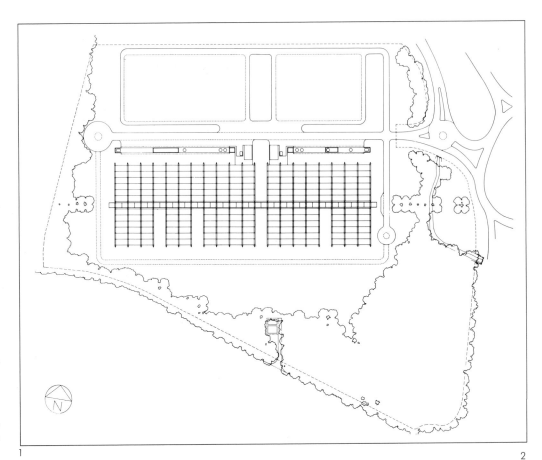

1

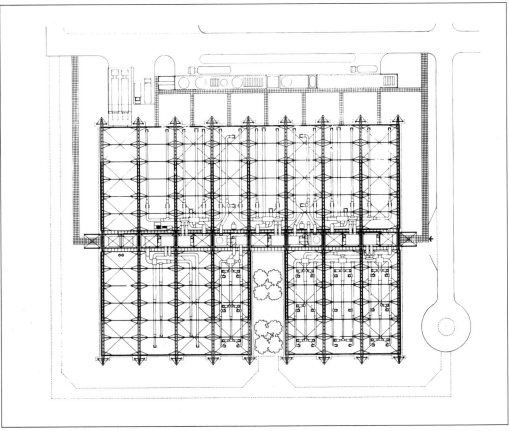

2

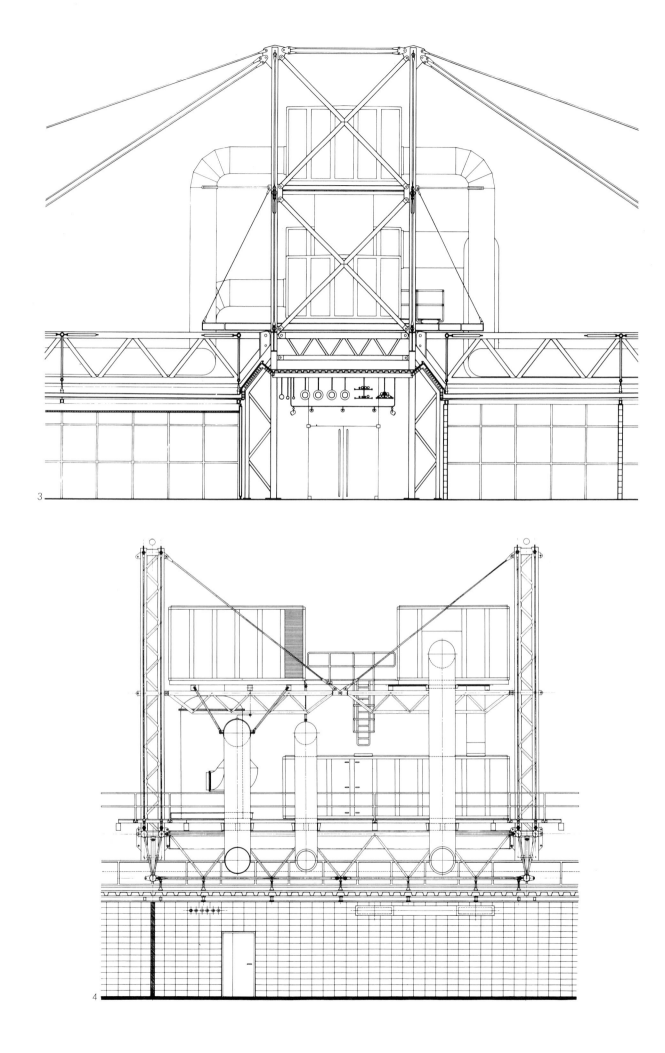

3

4

5

6

5. The open, rural site is an ideal setting for the High Tech style in its industrial mode.

6. Propped end of tension-assisted span, lattice steel beam.

7. The natural symmetry of circulation, structure, and services distribution gives the building a monumental quality.

8. External cladding is a standard grid with interchangeable panels.

7

8

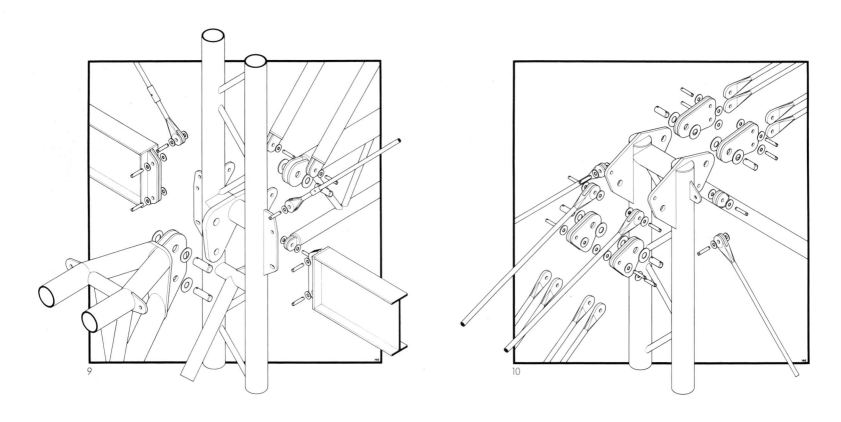

9

10

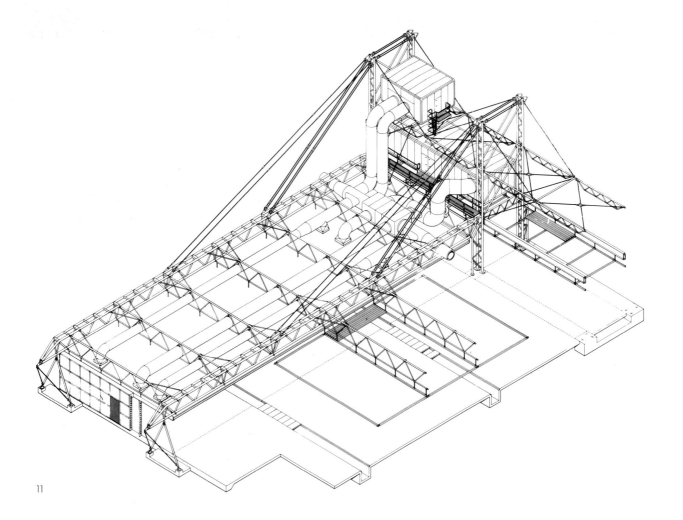

11

12

9, 10.   Exploded details of mast, beam and tension
rod connections: a full-size Meccano construction set.

11.   Isometric view of one structural bay showing
rooftop services distribution.

12.   Photograph of the main circulation spine, subject
of a hyper-realist painting by Ben Johnson.

Laboratories and Corporate Facility for PA Technology, Princeton, New Jersey
Architects: Richard Rogers Partnership
Completed 1984

The site is a level 10-acre plot (with an option on a further 16 acres for future development) on a new 100-acre industrial park six miles east of Princeton, New Jersey. Scattered developments in the surrounding countryside house a number of prestigious research and development facilities including RCA, J&J, Squibb, Exxon and Siemens.

PA Technology was established in North America in early 1980, housed in 10,760 sq.ft./1,000 m² of speculative office accommodation two miles east of Princeton town centre and five miles from the new site. By March 1982 the company had a staff of approximately 30 and a growth rate of one professional per month. The programme called for a custom-designed building offering maximum flexibility and permitting further growth.

Other requirements included a very high level of freedom of circulation and staff contact, flexibility in the arrangement of offices, labs and services, and a wide structural grid or totally free space. The north elevation, facing the main access to the site, was required to have a strong visual impact, expressing the company's innovative technology and high-quality image.

The design process resulted in a single-storey suspended steel structure, built rapidly from a kit of standard components fabricated off site. A central glazed arcade, 262'/80 m long and 26'/8 m wide, houses services, circulation and related activities. Open laboratory and office zones, including meeting rooms and administrative facilities, occupy 75'/22.8 m clear span spaces on either side. The services are located centrally over the spine in a bay-by-bay system that allows for future growth without major alteration or disruption of work areas, services, and plant rooms.

The first two phases total 64,600 sq.ft./6,000 m².

1

1. Side view showing roof-mounted plant: a simplified version of the Inmos building in South Wales.

2. Cut-away isometric view of roof.

3. The structural principle is similar to that of Inmos, but interpreted by a different engineer.

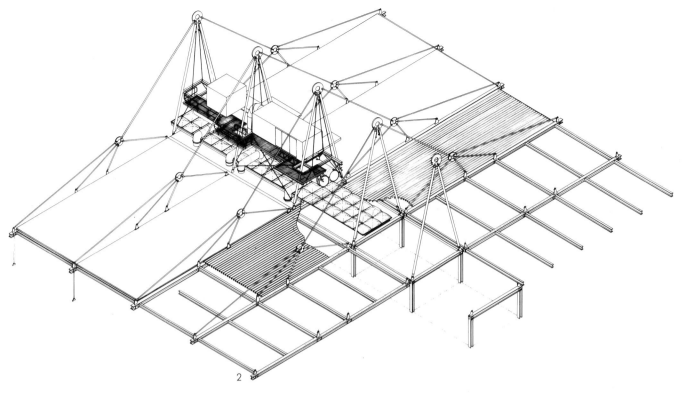

2

3

Laboratories and Corporate Facility for
PA Technology, Princeton, New Jersey

4. Cross section.

5. Plan.

6. A freestanding, infinitely extendable building, suitable only for open sites.

7. The random windows of Inmos here are rationalized into a single ribbon.

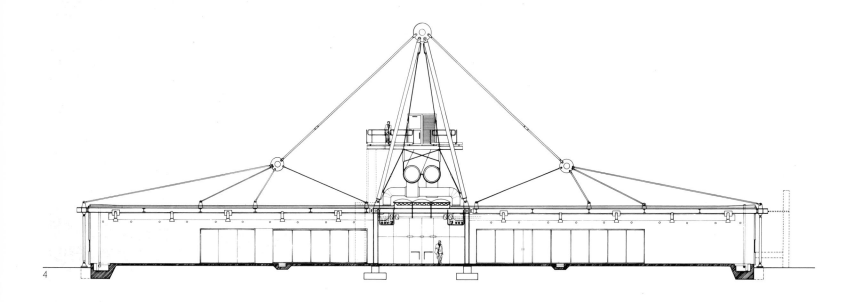

4

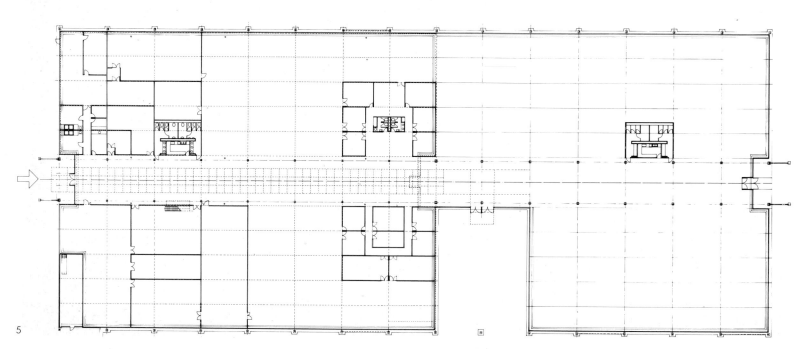

5

8   9   10

8. The glamour of High Tech transforms an industrial park into a "science park".

9. Primary colours: at Inmos, blue; at Princeton, red and yellow.

10. Central spine has a glazed roof so that the dramatic external structure can be admired from inside.

11.
High Tech architecture as a symbol of High Tech industry, though technically the two have little in common.

**Coin Street Development, South Bank, London
Architects: Richard Rogers Partnership
Project, not realized, design completed 1983**

The site is on the bend of the south bank of the Thames. The programme was developed in conjunction with the developer after detailed studies of the area. A comprehensive mixed development was recommended, including offices, housing, shopping, restaurants, leisure and light industry. The programme was also extended to include a pedestrian bridge, river pontoons, a glazed street, public open spaces, car parks and a service road.

The design is for an open-ended, flexible infrastructure capable of fostering a wide range of local and metropolitan activities for young and old from all walks of life. The scheme is based on a hierarchy of routes. The glazed pedestrian street acts as a covered link through the site from Waterloo Station to the river and across a footbridge to the North Bank. A network of open pedestrian routes, running parallel to and north-south across the glazed street, create a continuous link from the hinterland through the site to the river. The design allows for the embankment to be built out to a new line set up by the National Theatre, completing the river walk from Blackfriars to Waterloo Bridge.

Pedestrian movement and public activities are at ground level. The private offices are raised above the shopping and leisure facilities lining the glazed street. Four gateway pavilions, containing shopping and leisure activities, are located at the principal intersections with the glazed street. A large public open space is created on the river frontage, landscaped in the form of a sunken bowl to provide a sheltered environment for informal activities such as street theatre, funfairs, music, and circuses. Pontoons house typical pierhead activities such as marinas, historic ships, cafés, bars and restaurants.

The offices are divided into three clusters defined by the four gateway pavilions. Each cluster is broken down into linked office buildings with service zones at the hinge points. The atrium office building provides the glazed "galleria" space and combines energy efficiency with flexibility of use. The office buildings vary in height from 16 storeys on the river front to 7 at the centre, rising again to 13 at the Waterloo Bridge end. Most of the housing is located in 4-storey, south-facing courtyard family units fronting Stamford Street and the neighbouring community. There are also some flats with views over the river. The light-industrial area is below the glazed street.

Out of a total development area of 12.6 acres, less than 3% is used at ground level for offices and their related vertical services. The remaining 97% is given over to public activities.

The scheme was eventually abandoned after much public debate.

1

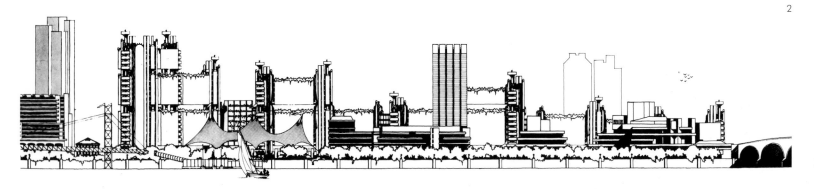

2

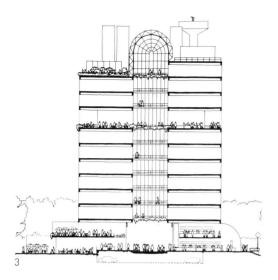

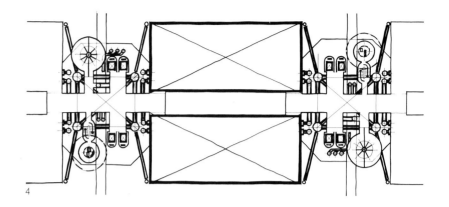

3

4

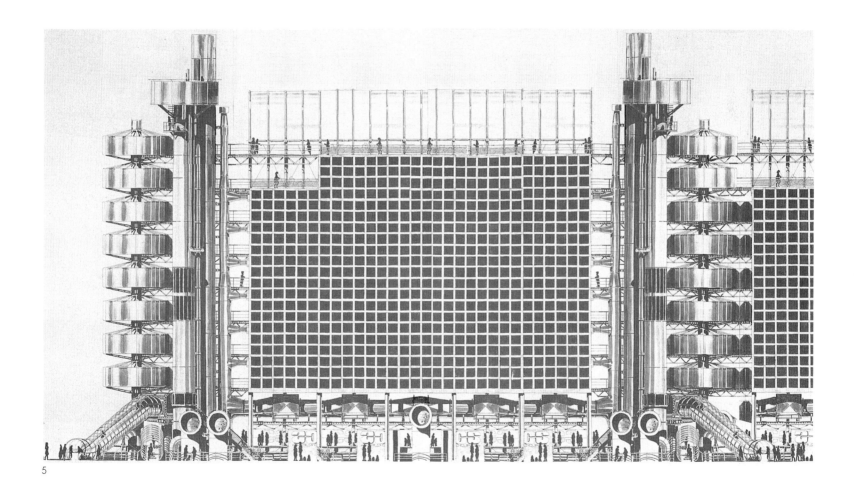

5

1. Model of the Coin Street megastructure, curving towards the river and a new pedestrian bridge.

2. Coin Street: elevation from the river.

3. Coin Street: cross section through "flexible infrastructure".

4. Diagrammatic plan showing service tower clusters.

39   5. Typical elevation.

New Thames bridge
Theoretical project
Architects: Richard Rogers Partnership
1986

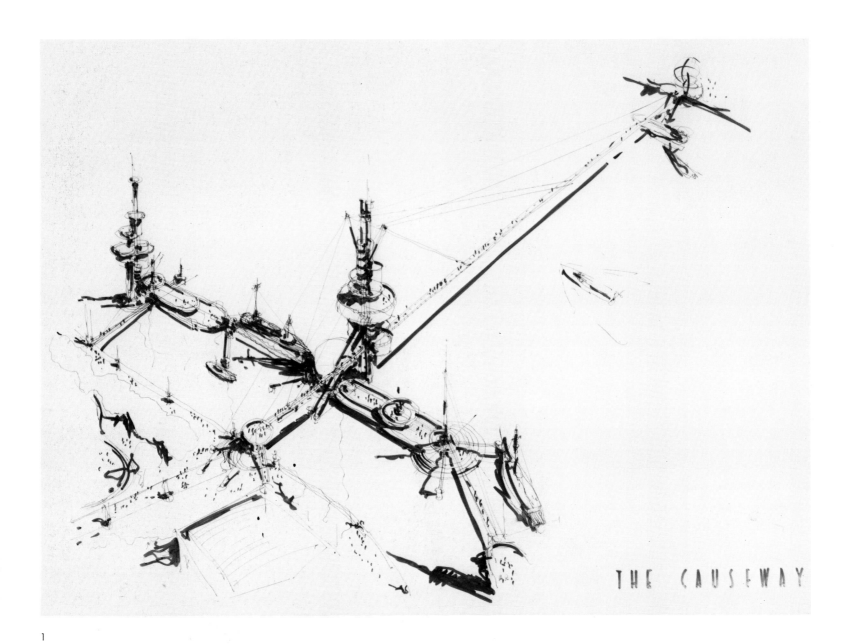

1

1. Theoretical proposal for a new Thames bridge.

2

3

2,3. The new Thames bridge was designed to
regenerate the South Bank by linking it directly to the
West End.

Lloyd's of London
Architects: Richard Rogers Partnership
Completed 1986

Lloyd's of London is located in the heart of the city's financial district. With the exception of the new square with the Commercial Union and P&O office towers to the north, the neighbouring streets and alleys are tight and winding, as if carved out of the solid building mass. In the surrounding area there are many places where developers and planners have replaced the small street network with tower blocks and large open pedestrian plazas. However, a conservation study, "Save the City", seriously questioned the formation of new open squares in a district where spaces are traditionally small and intimate.

Lloyd's of London dates back to the seventeenth century. It is now a vast market place and is considered a centre of world insurance. Lloyd's operates on the same principles as a traditional market. It is not a company, has no shareholders and accepts no corporate liability for the risks insured. It is a society of underwriters, formed into syndicates, who have stalls in Lloyd's market and agree on terms for accepting risks in whole or in part. Lloyd's efficiency depends upon a single market place under one roof. This is known as "The Room".

The Rogers design team summarized the requirements of the Lloyd's programme as follows:

to cater to the needs of the market into the twenty-first century, while retaining a single underwriting room up to three times the size of the existing Room;

to provide space for ancillary activities and essential tenants;

to maintain full continuity of trading with minimum disturbance;

to facilitate the flexible expansion and contraction of the underwriting space in line with future market trends, while creating a commercially viable office development;

to create a building of quality that not only contributes to the environment of the City of London but also maintains Lloyd's position as the centre of the world's insurance; and

to optimize the use of available land, allowing for a high degree of flexibility and choice of alternative uses during design, construction, and occupation of the building.

Lloyd's looks both inwards into its great atrium and outwards to six surrounding servant towers. These towers are intended to position the building in its urban context and enrich the city skyline. The architects maintain that the urban context was an important form generator. The servant towers stand outside the mass of the building, allowing the simple rectangular plan to make good use of the irregular site and to create a controlled framework within which the elevations can be changed in response to changing needs.

Whereas the frame of the building has a long life expectancy, the servant areas, filled with mechanical equipment, have a relatively short life. The equipment – mechanical services, lifts, toilets, kitchens, fire stairs and lobbies – sit loosely in the tower framework and are easily accessible for maintenance or replacement. The articulated servant towers express the faster rate of change of these elements. They are juxtaposed with the more permanent but equally legible "served" rectangle of the building. A strong tension is thus created between the dynamic parts and the permanent mass. Each technical component is separately expressed.

The main volume of the building is a series of 16-metre-wide concentric galleries overlooking a central atrium. Each gallery can be used either as part of the underwriting Room or as office space. Fixed obstructions such as toilets, stairs, entrances, lifts and columns are placed outside the main volume. The building is 12 storeys high on the north side (opposite the P&O and Commercial Union towers) and steps down to six storeys opposite the small-scale buildings to the south, creating terraces at various levels.

A total of twelve external glazed lifts offer magnificent views across London. All vertical movement within the underwriting Room is by escalators at the southern end of the atrium.

The floors are supported by reinforced concrete columns on a 35'x59'/10.8 m x 18 m grid. Each floor, designed to meet servicings as well as structural requirements, consists of a 6'/1.8 m grid of 22"x12"/ 550 mm x 300 mm beams supported on post-tensioned pre-stressed inverted "U" beams that span between brackets. The connection between floor and brackets is made using a yoke that transfers vertical loads to elastomeric bearings and horizontal loads to steel dowels. Overall lateral stability is provided by six sets of diagonal braces. Precast concrete stub columns at the floor grid intersections support steel permanent formwork for the floor slab, which in turn supports a raised access floor. The permanent formwork also provides support for services and sound-absorbent panels.

The six satellite towers consist of a precast concrete frame of columns, beams, and slabs. Four of the six towers carry large plant rooms located above roof level. The service towers are clad in stainless steel sandwich panels with a one-hour fire rating.

Main services run down the service towers and branch off horizontally at each level of the building. At the centre of each floor module of indirect lighting, sprinkler head, air conditioning terminal, smoke/heat sensor and acoustic treatment are integrated into a single element known as a rose.

1. Plan showing servant towers tucked into the irregularities of the site boundary.

Pages 44–45:

2. Rogers sees the "picturesque" profiles of the servant towers as a positive contribution to the urban scene.

3. View from the south showing the barrel vault over the central atrium.

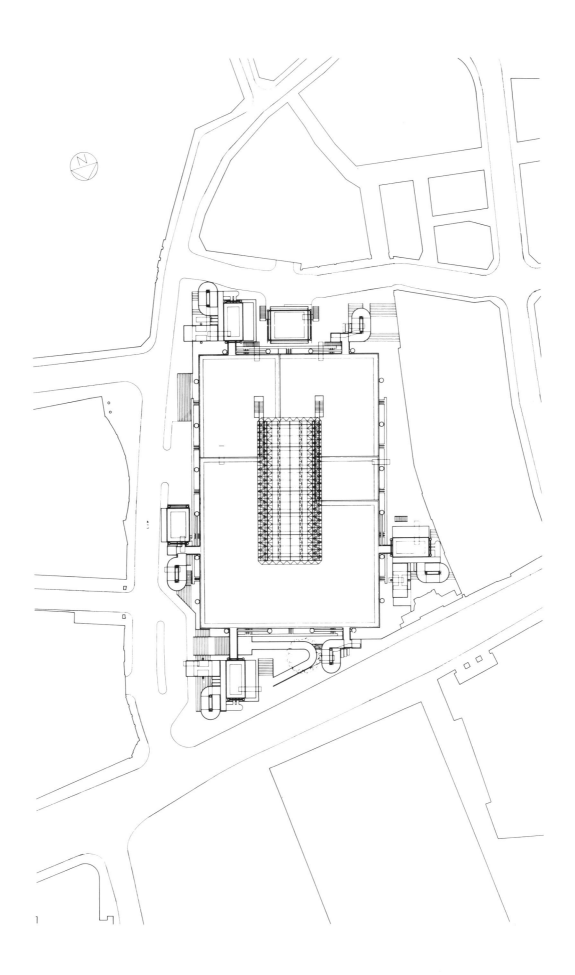

4

5

6

4. The simple box at the heart of the building is cut away so not to overshadow surrounding buildings.

5. Exposed steel structure of the atrium enclosure.

6. The old, conventionally classical, Lloyd's on the right; the new Lloyd's beyond.

7. In the foreground the Lloyd's building, with its services on the outside, including a stack of toilet modules. Beyond, the Commercial Union Building, with its services hidden away in a central core.

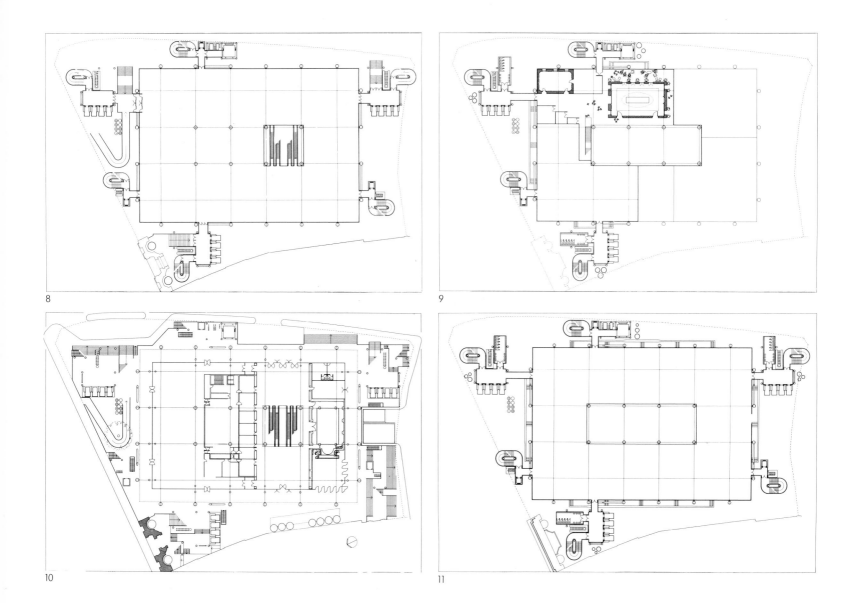

7

8. Ground floor plan.

9. Upper floor plan showing the Adam Room, transferred from the old building.

10. Basement plan.

11. Typical upper floor plan.

12. Cut away axonometric showing one level of "The Room".

13. The basement areas are intended to accommodate public facilities, such as shops and cafés.

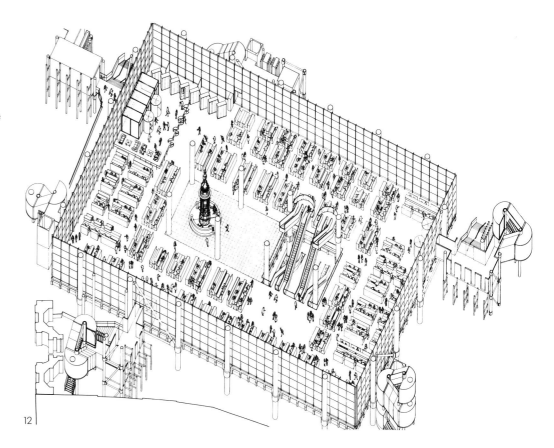

12

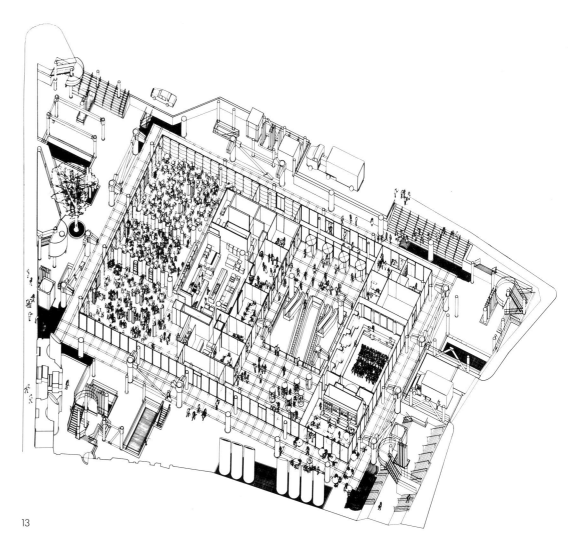

13

14. Cross section at an early stage in the development of the scheme. Plant rooms on top of the servant towers became much bigger.

15. The Lutine Bell standing in the central atrium.

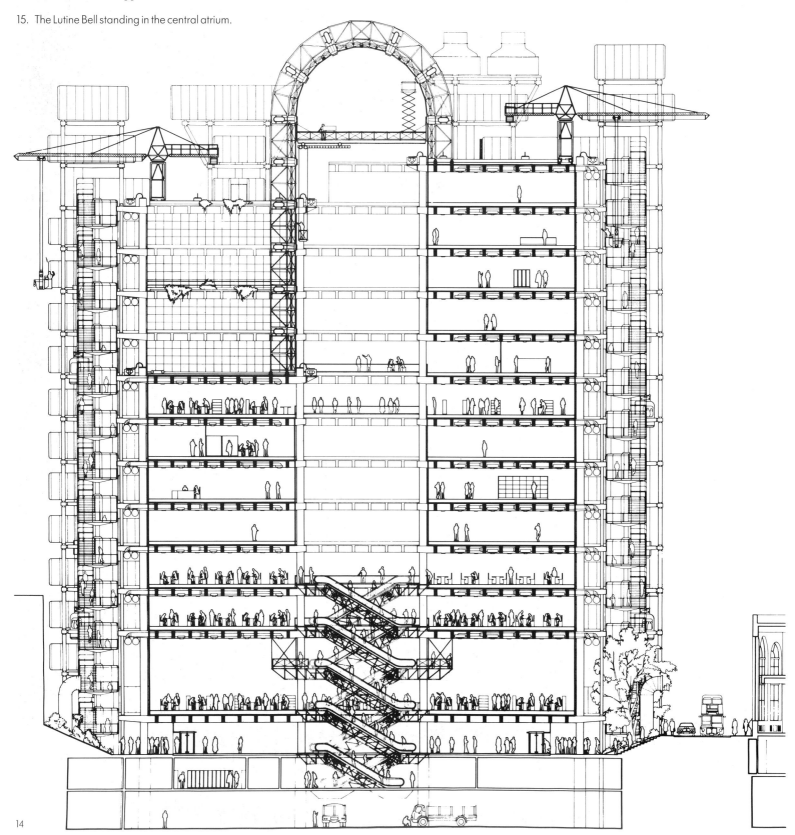

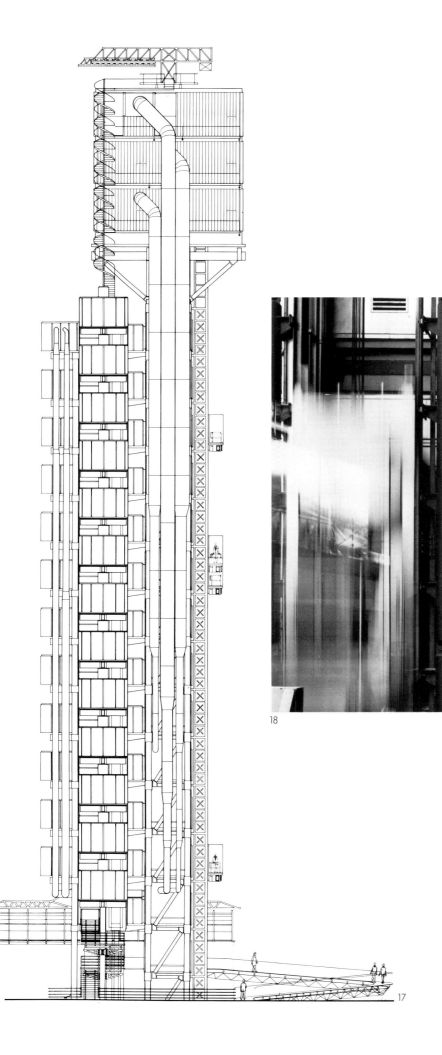

17

18

16. The main means of communication between the various levels of The Room is a bank of escalators in the atrium.

17. Elevation of a typical servant tower, with lifts on the right.

18. All passenger lifts are glazed, external "wall climbers", each with its own miniature air conditioning plant.

19., 20. Toilet modules were made in a factory and delivered complete to the site to be "plugged into" the building. They are not, however, unpluggable.

21. Detail of the external wall with "fishtail" air ducts.

22. Detail section through external wall.

23. Air ducts are slung from the building like exhaust pipes on a racing car.

19

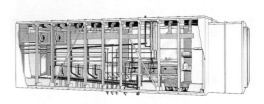

20

21

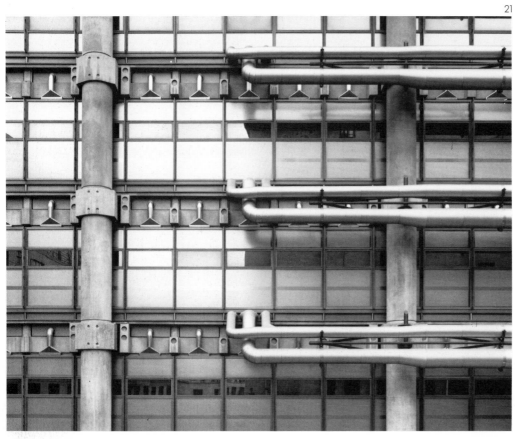

22

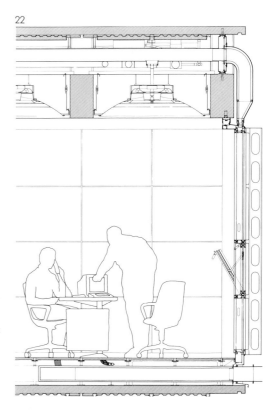

54

23

Headquarters for Willis, Faber and Dumas, Ipswich, East Suffolk
Architects: Foster Associates
Completed 1975

The Willis, Faber and Dumas concept diagram consists of two office floors, to accommodate about 1300 people, elevated and sandwiched between amenity/support areas above and below. At ground level there is a concourse, a swimming pool, a coffee bar, a gymnasium, mechanical and electrical plant, computers, and internal truck-loading docks. On the roof is a glass restaurant pavilion set in a landscaped garden. All floors are connected and penetrated by a landscaped atrium containing banks of escalators, and daylit by generously glazed roof.

Most office buildings have high standards for the visitor which become gradually diluted towards the user. The reverse is the case at Willis, Faber and Dumas . The entrance hall has an exposed concrete structure (emulsion painted), studded rubber flooring (the same as in the boiler room and lavatories) and demountable metal partitions (the same as everywhere else in the building). But the two office floors have carpet, custom-designed ceilings, and glare-free light fittings. All office space is open-plan.

The plan form and cross section of the building are a response to the need to relate a large new building to the fabric of a historic town. The deep plan allows the building to be low but still commercially viable. External walls are pushed right up to the site boundaries so that the original street pattern is reinforced. There are other advantages: fewer, larger floors make more efficient use of space, are more flexible, and consume less energy.

The 150 sq.ft./14 m² column grid was chosen as the most economical way to accommodate office planning constraints as well as larger spaces such as the swimming pool and truck-loading docks. A "necklace" of columns at the edge allows the external wall to follow the site boundaries. Floor slabs are flat, without downstand beams, so that their soffits can be exposed to view. The structure is thus very simple; it was easy to build and was the only site-based "wet" element. All other components were shop-fabricated for better quality control and speed of erection.

The suspended glass wall allows most users a view of the outside. Because the building is so deep, the heat loss at the perimeter has a relatively insignificant effect on energy loads. The architects at first found it hard to convince manufacturers and subcontractors of the feasibility of a curtain of glass suspended from the top edge of the building without mullions. Eventually, sufficient technical details and calculations were produced to demonstrate that it was not only feasible, but also reasonably cheap.

1

2

4

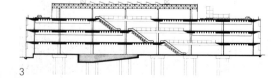

3

56

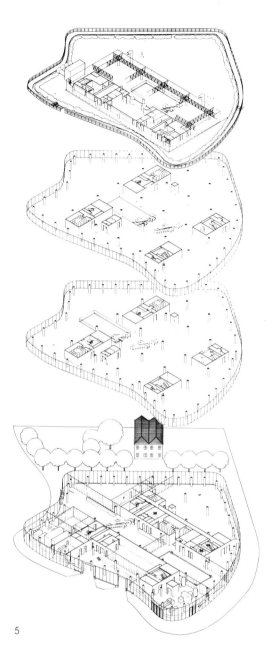

5

1., 2. The glass external wall is suspended like a curtain from the top edge of the building.

3. Section through atrium and basement swimming pool.

4. The top-lit atrium with cascading escalators has had a profound influence on British office design.

5. Exploded isometric. The curving external glass wall hugs the site boundary.

6. At night the reflections disappear and the interior is revealed.

6

**Sainsbury Centre for the Visual Arts, University of
East Anglia, Norwich
Architects: Foster Associates
Completed 1977**

The Sainsbury Centre combines two exhibition
galleries, a large reception conservatory, a school of
fine arts, a university faculty club, a 300-seat public
restaurant, and a basement with storage and workshop facilities. The design brings all the activities under
one roof. It is used for special exhibitions and, with
other parts of the campus, as an international conference centre.

The architects and their patrons visited several
galleries in Europe and the USA and identified the
following factors as important in the development of
the design: the positive qualities of tunable natural top
lighting; the importance of flexibility for change and
growth; the need for good security that was not labour
intensive; the value of usable storage space; the need
to service a gallery without disturbing either exhibits or
users; a desire to respect and integrate social elements; and a need to see the display and furniture as
totally coordinated elements of the overall design.

The building is mainly factory produced, the work on
site being virtually confined to the assembly of prefabricated components. High technology is equated in
this building with low energy. Any part of the external
walls and roof can be changed in minutes to give any
combination of glazed, solid or louvred aluminium
panels. A sub-frame of extruded aluminium receives
the 45′x45′/1.8x1.2 m panels. These are joined together by Neoprene gaskets that double as continuous gutters discharging into a cast-aluminium grille at
the base of the building. The external panels marked
the first use in the building industry of vacuum-formed
superplastic aluminium. The end walls are full height
24′/7.3 m glass panels joined with clear silicone adhe-
sive.

Towers and trusses house all services, toilets, and
ancillary spaces, and provide freeways for lighting
installations and maintenance. The entire inner wall
and ceiling lining is a tunable system of perforated
aluminium louvres. These are motorized and linked
with external and internal light sensors to control light
levels automatically. Artificial lighting is based on
extruded aluminium lighting tracks. The combination
of these systems provides virtually infinite flexibility
without the need to disrupt the layout at gallery floor
level. The substructure and spine basement are reinforced concrete.

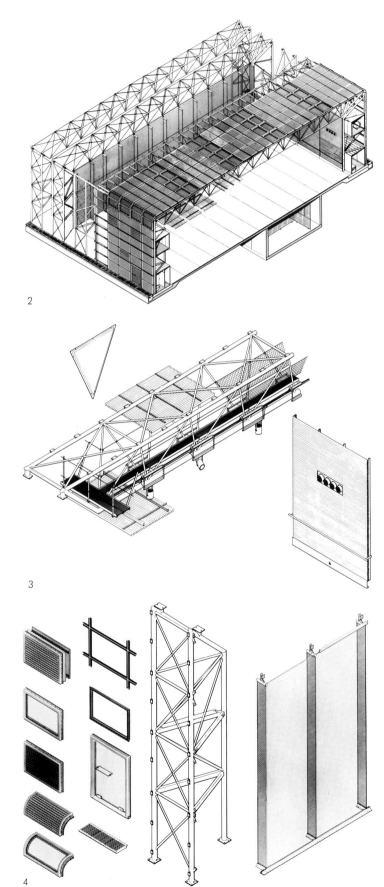

2

3

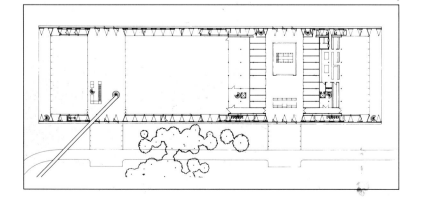

1

4

58

5

6

1. Plan. The cellular spaces to the right are internal offices.

2. Isometric analysing the main building elements.

3. Lattice beam with access walkway and internal lining wall with air outlets.

4. Kit of parts: cladding components, structural column and all-glass end wall.

5., 6. The cladding systems envelop the whole building, including the roof.

7. Entrance to the basement storage areas.

8. The completely undifferentiated space of the interior has been criticized as a setting for works of art.

9. A temple to art.

Hammersmith Centre, London
Architects: Foster Associates
Project, not realized, design completed 1977

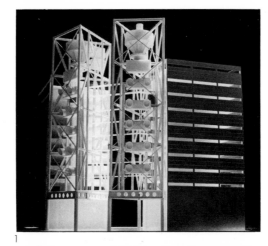

Hammersmith is a thriving London Borough four miles from the West End and ten miles from Heathrow Airport. In recent years it has been subject to stress and change through new building developments and new roads that penetrate the area to link up with motorways to the Airport and the West. London Transport is the owner of the prime remaining site in the heart of the district. At present it contains a mixture of low-grade structures, an outdated bus garage, an underground railway station, and no public open space. Surrounded by heavy traffic, it is probably one of the busiest intersections in Europe.

The scheme was designed for a balance of bus and underground transportation, office development, and new road planning to create an urban centre extending through to a new Town Park alongside. The heart of the site is dominated by the large-scale transportation elements, the roofs of which form a four-acre public space. One of the options puts a clear-span enclosure at the upper level using new generation architectural fabrics. The social, commercial, and energy implications of this proposal involved extensive research, which the architects believe has confirmed an exciting potential to recreate human space within an urban fabric fragmented by traffic.

1. Detailed model of corner service tower.

2. Model showing the four-acre suspended fabric roof.

3. Section. The roof of the transport interchange forms a public open space.

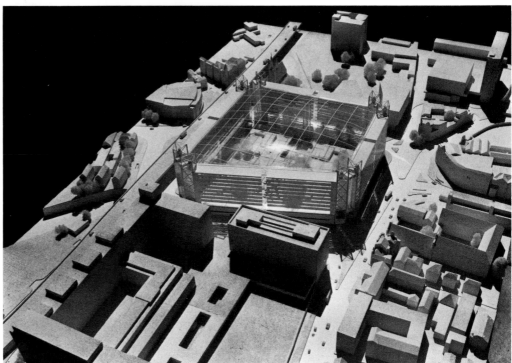

1

2

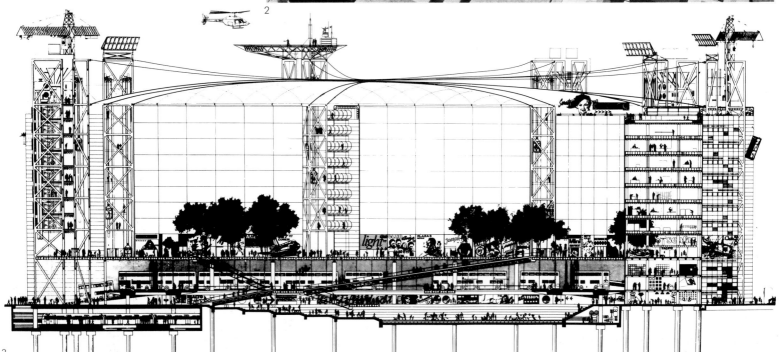

3

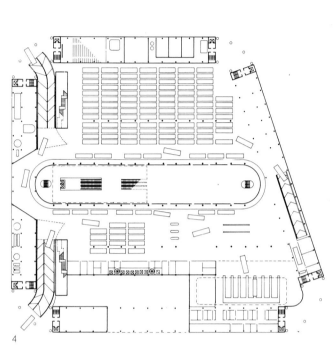

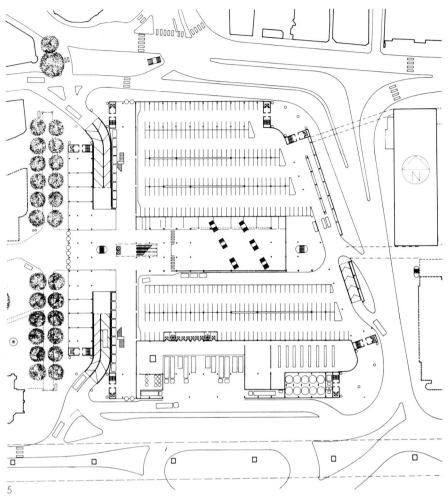

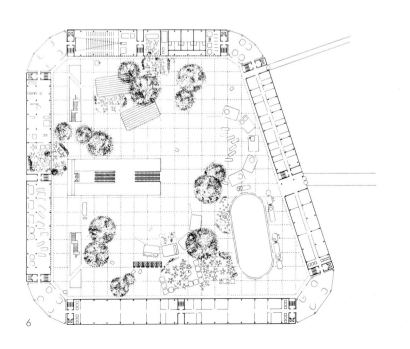

4. Bus station plan.

5. Car park plan.

6. Plan of public open space surrounded by four
linear buildings with service towers at the corners.

**Warehouse and Distribution Centre for Renault,
Swindon, Wiltshire
Architects: Foster Associates
Completed 1983**

Renault wanted to establish a progressive image of design quality not only in its product range but also in the working environment. Excellence was to be sought within demanding limits of time and cost, and in ways that would accommodate change during the life of the building.

The site is an irregular, sloping plot of 6.5 hectares on the western edge of Swindon, a fast-growing town with good rail and road links to London. The design concept integrates responses to the programme and the site by using a module that can fill out the site irregularities and allow for random growth.

From the outside the building form is articulated by the modules and their expressed structures. Each module is 91'/24 m square in plan, 25'/7.5 m high at the edge rising to 31'/9.5 m at the apex, and suspended from 52'/16 m high masts. The first phase is of 42 modules, which accommodate a warehouse, distribution, and regional offices with computer installations, a showroom for cars and trucks, and an after-sales maintenance engineering training school with associated workshops and seminar rooms, a restaurant and an entrance canopy.

The structural frame is of arched steel beams suspended at their quarter points from pre-stressed circular rolled hollow steel masts. Connection points are provided on the suspension structure so that the initial building ground plan can be extended by 67% without major disruption. The floor construction is of reinforced concrete with an accurately-levelled granolithic topping. The roof covering consists of a continuous solvent-welded, reinforced PVC membrane above 2.6"/75 mm mineral wool insulation.

A clear glass panel at each column combines the benefits of natural light with views of the structural masts and tension rods. At the apex of each module there is a further rooflight of double skin translucent UPVC louvres that can be opened for summer ventilation or automatic smoke venting. The special external wall panels are of expanded polyurethane foam insulation between two skins of steel. Glazing to the wall and rooflights uses the Pilkington "Planar" system — an assembly of armourplate glass suspended on bolts countersunk into the thickness of the glass.

The building is heated by a central gas-fired boiler plant that feeds warm air unit heaters and air handling units. Lighting in the warehouse uses high-pressure sodium lamps; the workshops have fluorescent fittings, and special tungsten lighting is provided in the showroom and offices. The office, showroom, and restaurant furniture is a combination of special systems designed by the architects, proprietary chairs and storage units, and some items re-used from other Renault facilities.

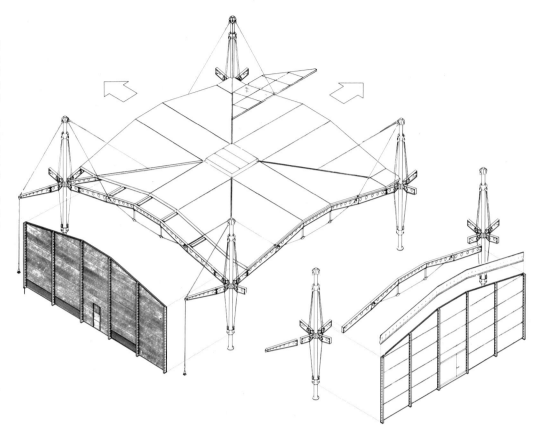

1. Isometric of one structural bay.

2. Site plan.

3. For Norman Foster, this is an uncharacteristically flamboyant structure.

4. Entrance hall and showroom.

5. Functionally and conceptually, Foster's Renault distribution centre is similar to Rogers' Fleetguard distribution centre (see p. 22).

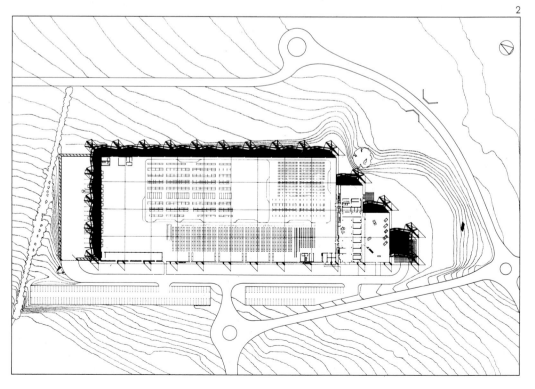

2

3

4

5

Airport Terminal, Stansted, Essex
Architects: Foster Associates
Project, design completed 1986

In accordance with the British Airports Authority's master plan for Stansted Airport, the new terminal is situated on the opposite side of the runway from the existing terminal.

All public facilities are provided on a single concourse floor, with arrivals and departures side by side. The landside vehicle forecourt and passenger set-down are constructed at the same level as the main concourse. The short-term car park and coach station are situated to the south of the forecourt, set at a lower level to minimize visual impact and give easy access into the terminal from below the forecourt. The proposed British Rail station is located below the landside forecourt as an extension of an undercroft that runs beneath the entire concourse level. Passengers proceed through the check-in area, security and immigration controls and departure lounge to a tracked transit station on the same level. From here automatic tracked vehicles transport passengers to satellite buildings from which they board aircraft.

The main function of the undercroft is to service the concourse level. It contains the baggage handling systems, all the engineering plant for the building, the vehicle servicing area, and storage. There are no engineering services at roof level. The supports for the roof form tree-like structures, on a 387 sq.ft./36 m² grid, comprising clusters of four connected tubular steel columns. The roof is made up of lattice-shell domes. Each dome rises to a height of 9.8'/3 m above eaves level giving an overall maximum external height above concourse level of 49.2'/15 m. All distribution equipment for heating, ventilation, air conditioning, and lighting serving the concourse is contained within the clusters of steel columns.

All passenger facilities at concourse level that require enclosure, such as shops, banks, kitchens, left luggage, lavatories and medical facilities, have been designed as freestanding demountable structures.

Natural light for the concourse is provided by the glazed cladding and the rooflights in the lattice domes. After dark, the concourse will be lit indirectly by light reflected from the internal surface of the roof.

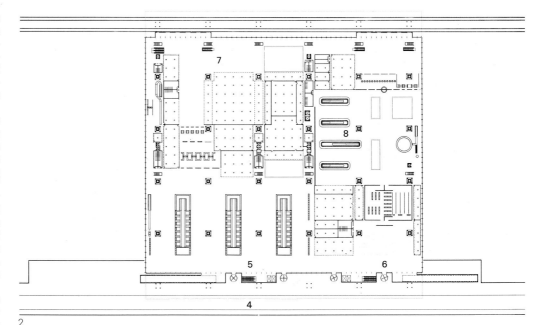

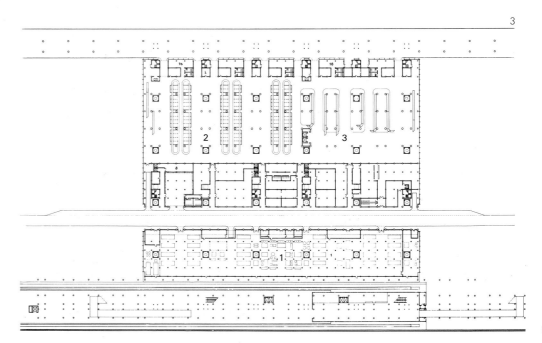

1. Section.

2. Concourse plan.

3. Basement plan.
Key: 1 central plant, 2 departures baggage hall, 3 arrivals baggage hall, 4 access road, 5 departures hall, 6 arrivals hall, 7 departure lounge, 8 immigration central.

4

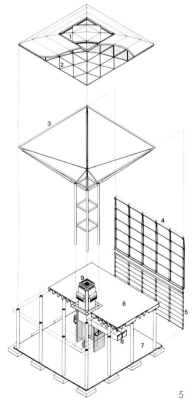

6

4. This is an understated, low-profile building, quite unlike Renault.

5. Detail, exploded isometric.
Key: 1 integral rooflight, 2 steel roof lattice shell and finish, 3 steel structural "tree", 4 glazing to concourse areas, 5 cladding to basement areas, 6 concrete concourse floor, 7 concrete basement floor, 8 air distribution, 9 indirect lighting and environmental services.

6. The transparency of the building makes its plan easily intelligible to travellers.

5

HongkongBank Headquarters, Hong Kong
Architects: Foster Associates
Completed 1986

The headquarters of the HongkongBank is a 47-storey, 590'/180 m high building in the heart of Hong Kong's rapidly growing business district. The site has been occupied by the Bank since the middle of the nineteenth century. Its previous building, completed in 1935, was, in its day, the tallest and most sophisticated building in Asia. The new building, like its predecessor, faces Statue Square, one of central Hong Kong's few remaining public open spaces. Flanked on the east side by the old Supreme Court Building (which now houses Hong Kong's legislative assembly) and on the north side by the Star Ferry terminal and the harbour, the square provides the bank a dramatic setting.

The building contains the main Hong Kong retail banking hall, administrative departments for local and worldwide operations, vaults, foreign exchange dealing rooms, and a computer centre. It differs fundamentally from the conventional concrete frame and glass curtain wall structures that have come to characterize Hong Kong and every other modern city in the developed world. Its plan, form, structure, materials, and method of construction are all unique.

The building's overall shape is not that of a simple rectangular or circular tower like most high-rise buildings. Instead, it has a more complex form, made up of three visually distinct bays. These bays rise to different heights to conform to the setback requirements of Hong Kong's building regulations, which are aimed at preventing the overshadowing of neighbouring streets. The building is limited to 35 storeys on Des Voeux Road and 28 on Queen's Road, with only the central bay rising to the full 47 storeys.

The main front and rear elevations are entirely glazed with floor to ceiling windows maximizing the views to sea and up to The Peak. But the two narrower sides, where the service runs and escape stairs have been concentrated, have a quite different, more deeply modelled profile. To the east, overlooking Bank Street, the building regulations have once again caused the building to step back as it rises.

The three bays are suspended over a completely unobstructed plaza on the ground floor, which is an extension of Statue Square. It is open to pedestrians 24 hours a day, but retracting screens can provide protection in case of typhoons. Instead of a conventional front entrance, the banking hall is entered by one of a pair of escalators that rises from the middle of the plaza. Passersby can look up into the 10-floor-high atrium through a glass "underbelly". Two arrays of mirrors, one fixed to the outside of the building, the other hanging in the top of the atrium, reflect sunlight down through the middle of the building to the plaza below. The outside "sunscoop" is motorized and programmed by computer to track the changing elevation of the sun. Below the plaza there are four basement levels for more public banking facilities, vaults, and plant rooms.

The complexity of the exterior reflects the variety of the interior spaces. Apart from the galleried atrium, double-height spaces are distributed throughout the building. These are there partly for structural reasons but also to accommodate semi-public and social functions, such as staff recreation, executive dining, conference rooms, and VIP reception. Because of the

different heights of the three bays, the floor plan changes as the tower rises. Public areas are at the base while the smaller floors at the top of the building lend themselves more readily to executive functions. Conventional high-rise buildings rely heavily on lifts for circulation. But waiting for them can cause considerable irritation. Consequently, the express lifts in the HongkongBank serve only the five double-height floors; communication within the zones is by escalators. This requires fewer lifts and cuts down waiting time. There is also a greater feeling of integration and communication between floors.

One of the most striking features of the building is its exposed steel structure divided into five vertical zones. Using a structural system derived from bridge construction, each zone is made up of a stack of lightweight steel and concrete floors that are hung from exposed steel suspension trusses at the double-height floors. These are in turn supported by two rows of steel masts and are braced against wind forces by lateral cross-bracing in each of the zones. Each of the masts is itself made up of four tubular columns, linked at every floor by rectangular Vierendeel steel sections. The steelwork was fabricated by the British Steel Corporation and shipped to Hong Kong in sections. The structural arrangement of the Bank does away with the need for a concrete central core. Instead, each floor is completely open between the two rows of masts. A clear span of over 108'/33 m is interrupted only by a single row of steel hangers. This degree of openness allows for maximum flexibility in the arrangement of the interior. Prefabricated service

continued on page 83 ▶

1

1. The HongkongBank has a powerful urban presence, though it is by no means the tallest building on the island.

2. The "incomplete" look of the building is typical of the High Tech style, implying that it might be extended or even partially dismantled.

Pages 70–71:

3., 4. Site plan and section. Norman Foster has always seen the real site for the building as the complete strip of land from the ferry terminal to the Botanical Gardens.

5. Statue Square, on the north side of the building, is almost the only urban public open space in Hong Kong.

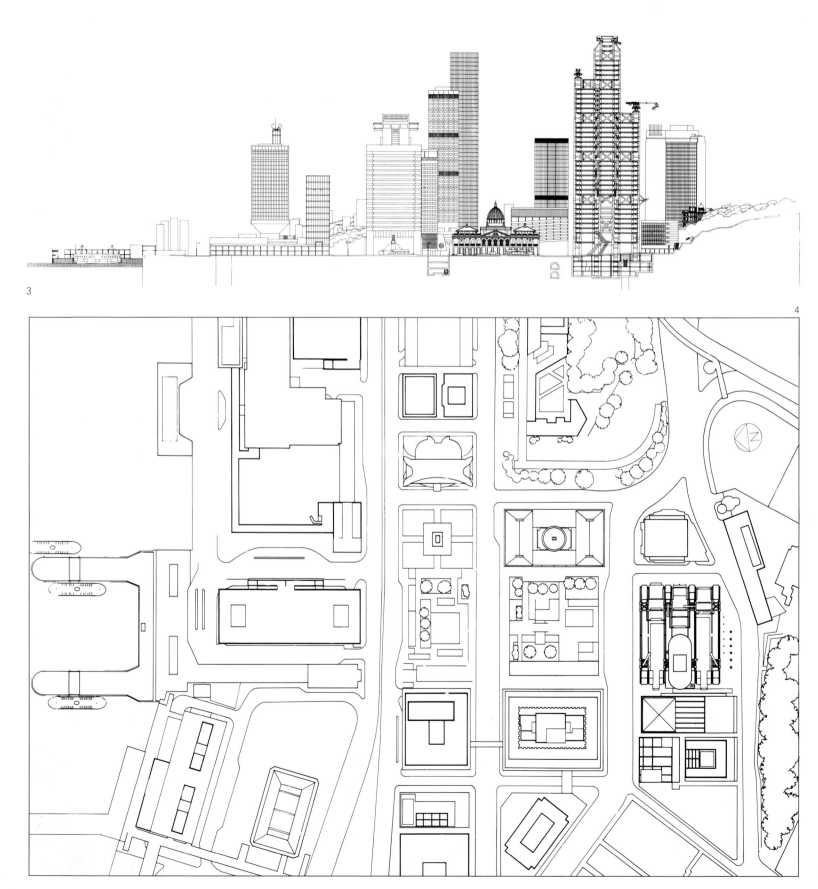

3

4

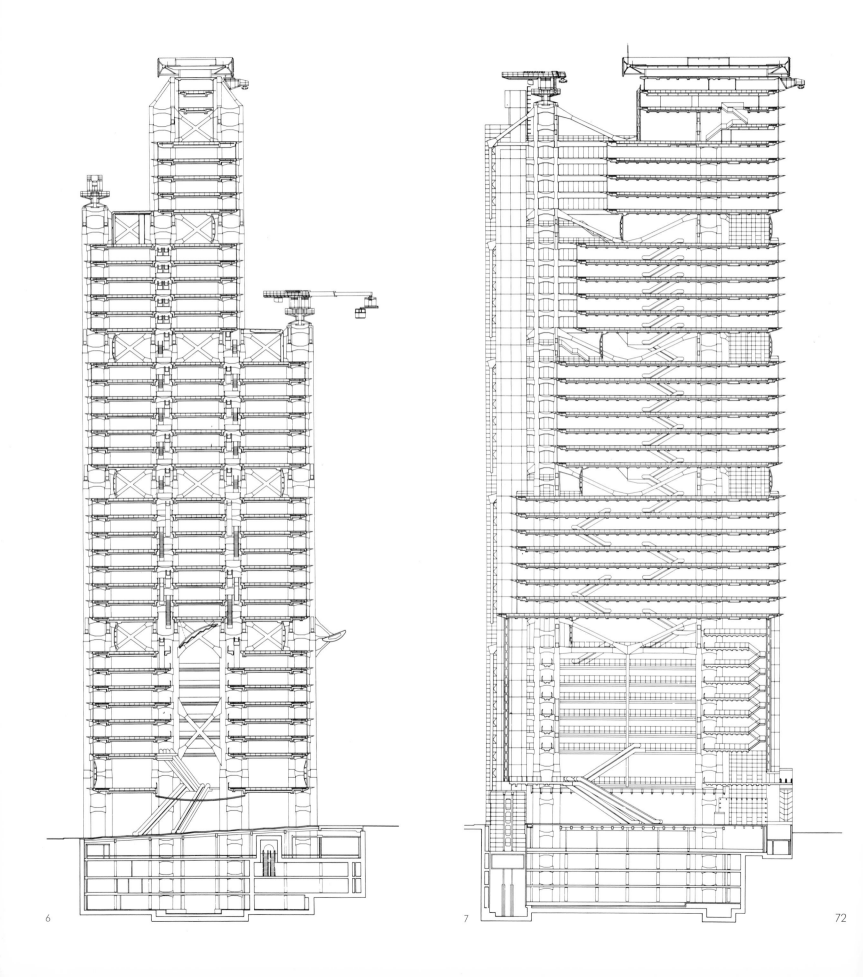

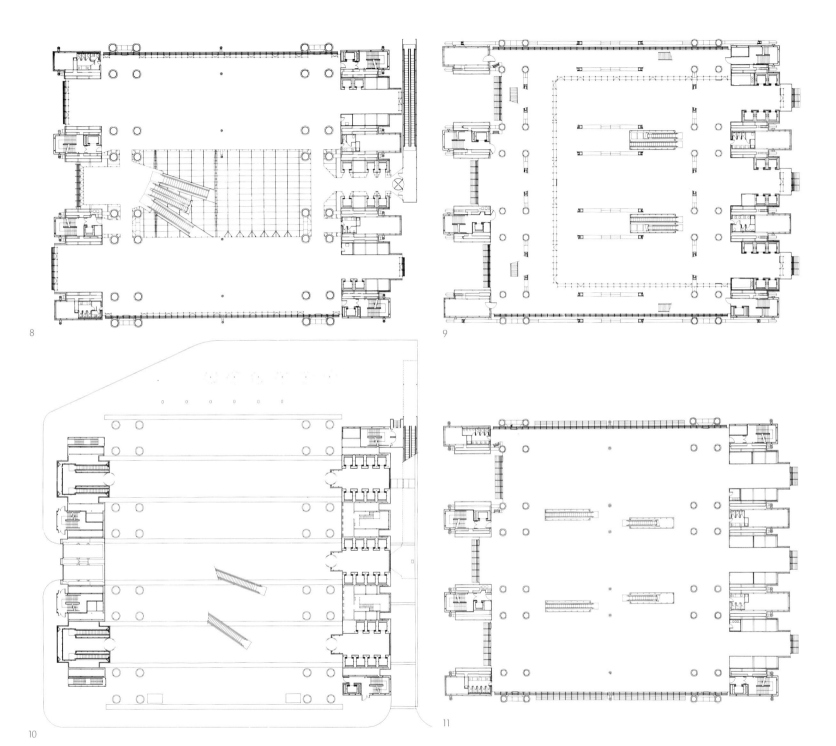

8

9

10

11

6. North-south section.

7. East-west section, showing setbacks to comply with local planning regulations.

8. Plan, banking hall level.

9. Plan, typical double height floor.

10. Plan, plaza (ground) level.

11. Typical floor plan.

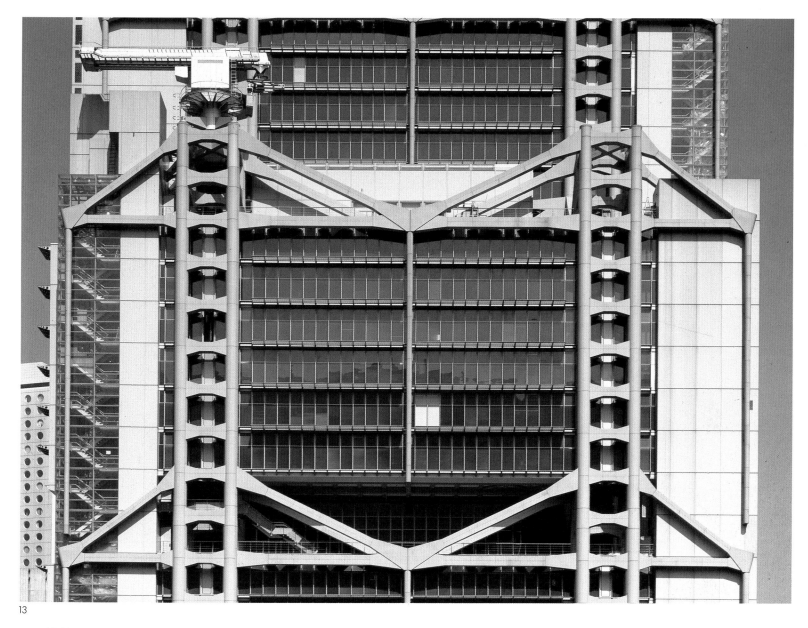

13

12. Lift lobbies alternate with stacks of service modules on the west (left) side of the building.

13., 14. Floors are suspended from the 2-storey high "coat-hangers".

Captions to illustrations on pp. 76–79 appear on p. 80.

14

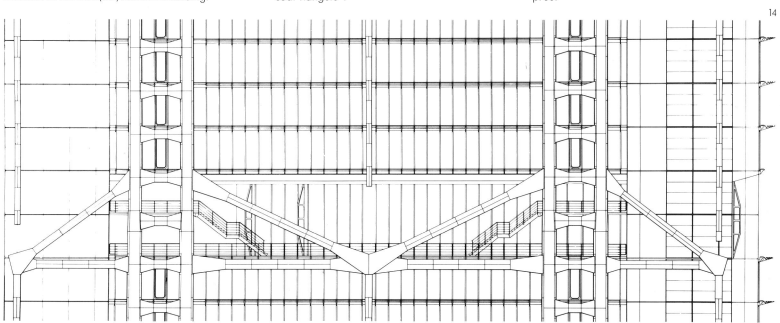

19

20

Pages 76–77:

15. The central atrium, looking east towards the so-called "cathedral wall", with escalators emerging through the glass underbelly from the plaza below.

16. The underbelly is a lightweight steel structure on the catenary or "rope bridge" principle.

Pages 78–79:

17. Escalator landing at the upper banking hall level.

18. Open galleries overlook the atrium and, through the glass underbelly, the plaza.

19., 20. Internal half of the "sun scoop", suspended in the top of the atrium like an aeroplane in a museum.

21., 22. The external bank of mirrors is motorized and computer-controlled to track the sun.

23

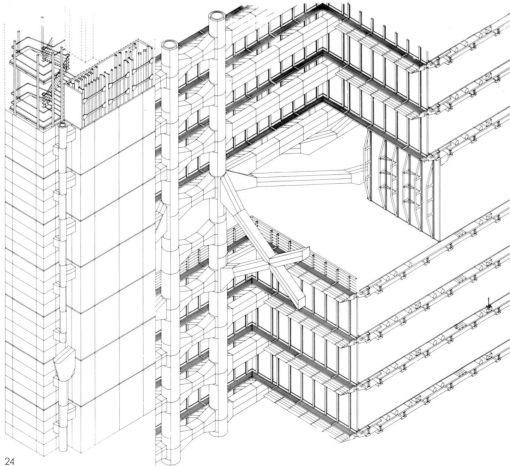

24

23. Double-height storeys at particular intervals in the building accommodate social uses such as restaurants and recreation areas.

24. Cut-away isometric showing external terrace at double-height storey.

25. Maintenance crane on top of one of the massive steel masts.

26. Plan at level 41: private dining room.

modules and escape stairs, hung from the outer ends of the suspension trusses, balance the weight of the main floors.

Electrical and air conditioning distribution services are accommodated under a raised floor rather than above a suspended ceiling, where alteration would be more difficult. Outlets for telephones, computers, electricity cables, and air conditioning can be altered simply by relocating one of the lightweight, honeycomb, aluminium floor panels. The construction of these panels was borrowed from aircraft industry technology. External cladding is a specially developed aluminium system made by Cupples of St Louis, Missouri, and is finished in three shades of grey. The building was designed to be built as quickly as possible and to the highest standards of quality. As much as possible of the building was prefabricated in factories in Europe, America, and Japan, and assembled on site. The on-floor services, for example, are contained in 139 prefabricated modules that not only contain air conditioning and electrical plant but also toilets. These modules were fitted with everything, including mirrors and soap dishes, before they left the factory in Japan.

The building was designed to meet the exacting functional and technical demands of one of the world's leading financial institutions, well into the next century. Its architecture is meant to reflect the status of the Bank and its confidence in the future of Hong Kong as the world's third largest financial centre.

25

26

28

29

27. Aluminium *brises-soleil* double as access walkways for maintenance of the curtain wall.

28. Basement entrance lobby on the east side of the building.

29. Elaborately expressive canopy over a secondary entrance on the west side of the building.

Office Building for Digital at Aztec West, Bristol, Gloucester
Architects: Nicholas Grimshaw and Partners
Completed 1982

The building contains 32,280 sq.ft./3,000 m² of office space on two floors. This is the first phase of a two-phase development that will eventually double the accommodation and extend the building to form a complete square with a central courtyard.

The design incorporates several special features to accommodate the rapidly changing requirements of the High Tech office user.

The general arrangement of served and servant spaces, with the latter outside the main volume, reduces costs, gives a much better net to gross ratio (92%), gives natural ventilation to toilets and escape stairs, allows the construction to suit the function without compromise, and leaves the main area completely free and unobstructed.

The structure is based on a 155 sq.ft./14.4 m² module with columns on a 24'/7.2 m grid and pairs of primary beams at first floor and roof level. This allows the structure to be extended in either direction without affecting the existing building. It also reduces the depth of structural elements and hence the height of the service zones.

The main building envelope is clad entirely in double-glazed mirrored units with relocatable operable windows. Half of the skin has opaque insulation panels zipped to the inside of the cladding grid, which allows instant relocation of window and wall without affecting weather tightness.

Power and telecommunication distribution is by fully accessible floor lines on a 8'/2.4 m grid.

Heating and ventilation are based on a ceiling void/plenum system with secondary fans mounted in interchangeable ceiling tiles to pull warm air down where necessary.

Lighting is by mobile, high-efficiency, floor-standing uplights to give variable lighting conditions when and where required without affecting the ceiling layout.

1

2

1., 2. Small factory/office buildings on suburban sites are the staple diet of High Tech. Often the clients are High Tech businesses, in the industrial sense.

3. Ground and first floor plans.

4. The articulated staircase tower is a miniature exercise in High Tech composition.

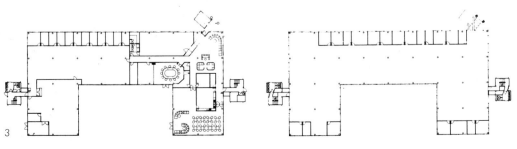

3

Warehouse for Herman Miller, Chippenham, Wiltshire
Architects: Nicholas Grimshaw and Partners
Completed 1983

The most interesting feature of this 75,000 sq.ft./ 7,000 m² distribution warehouse, on a green field site just outside Chippenham, is its metal cladding system. Client Herman Miller, the multi-national furniture manufacturer, first introduced the idea that an office work station be conceived and marketed as an integrated kit of interchangeable parts. It seemed appropriate that this philosophy should be adopted for the cladding of the new warehouse, especially since the building would be seen by countless businessmen from a nearby embankment of the London/Bristol inter-city railway line. Herman Miller allowed the architects to develop an entirely new cladding system, using the warehouse as a prototype. The building was handed over in April 1983 within budget and at a unit cost of $ 34.20/£ 22.52 per square foot.

The system gives the client considerable operational flexibility. Solid wall panels, window panels, doors and fire doors can be unbolted and moved to any location on a 4'x8'/2.4x1.2 m grid. The four apertures of each window frame can be infilled with a variety of secondary components such as ventilation louvres, hoods containing external floodlights and hoods allowing neat pipe inlets. The "Meccano"-like appearance of many of the purely functional elements, such as stiffening ribs and bolt heads, add visual interest, especially in strong sunlight.

The system is supported by pairs of Unistrut channels (standard components that allow bolted fixings anywhere along their length). Continuous extruded strips of black Neoprene slotted between each pair provide the weather seal at each vertical panel joint. Higher panels overlap lower ones, like vertical tile hanging, and each joint is stiffened by a special "T" bar that doubles as a ladder rail for window cleaning. Internally, insulation and sound absorption are achieved by separate perforated steel liner trays and rockwool slabs. The resulting airspace between inner and outer skins means that the wall has all the advantages of a traditional cavity wall. All external components are enamel coated, except for the bolts, which are stainless steel.

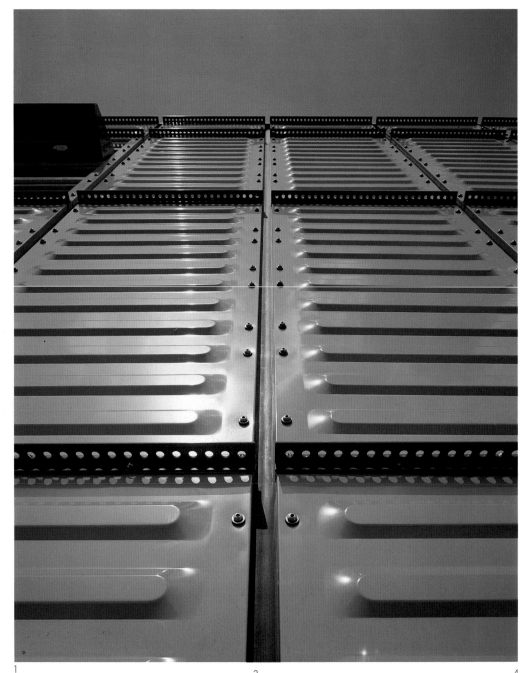

2   1   3   4

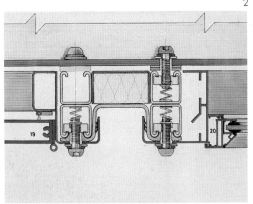

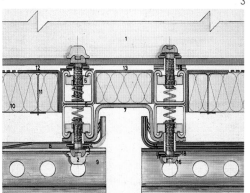

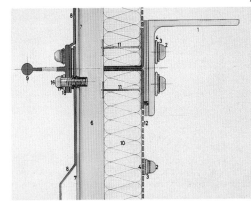

5

6   7

1. The cladding system was developed from scratch. Panels of different types can be unbolted and moved to any position on a standard grid.

2.–4. Architect's technical drawings of the cladding system.

5. The rounded corner is a characteristic Grimshaw detail.

6. Glazed link between blocks.

7. Inside the warehouse. It is easy to see why so much design effort should have been concentrated on the cladding.

IBM Sports Hall, Hursley Park, Hampshire
Architects: Nicholas Grimshaw and Partners
Completed 1982

The building is located in the grounds of the IBM laboratories at Hursley Park just outside Winchester. The programme was for a multi-purpose sports hall for the social club. The hall was to be for badminton and other indoor sports, but also for occasional social functions. The budget was low and the building was to be capable of future expansion, which is reflected in the positioning of the building and the planning of the services.

Having researched sports buildings, the architects felt that the usual brick box was neither desirable nor appropriate in such a setting. The most striking element of the design is the external structural framework, which consists of five tubular steel trussed portal frames at 17'/5.25 m centres spanning 59'/18 m. This arrangement results in a clear, flush-walled space inside. The structure breaks down the bulk of the building both by the articulation of the frames themselves and by the patterns their shadows cast on the silver cladding.

The cladding panels are self-finished, foam-cored, steel-skinned sandwich panels bolted to cleats welded to the main frame and the gable mullions. The mullions have been detailed so that the entire gable wall can be unbolted and taken down. This allows extension along the building's east/west axis, which could then include prefabricated squash courts and additional play floor space.

Eaves and corners are formed from curved double-skinned translucent blue panels, that give a neutral internal light without glare. From the outside, the translucent panels glow at night when the lights are on.

The roof is suspended at the node points of the trusses with special hanger assemblies using "nodus pin" cast steel connectors, manufactured by British Steel, and coupling boxes to allow individual adjustment. The roof is a lightweight metal deck with insulation board, covered with a single-welded PVC membrane. The use of PVC components allowed the complicated upstands at the connectors to be easily formed and sealed.

The interior of the building is open and flush-walled to give the maximum clear space for sport. The floor is sprung beech. Temperature and ventilation are maintained by two external heat pumps slung in cradles from the main frame. Air ducts are exposed and power cables are all accommodated in one high-level, face-fixed duct. The individual connections to the lights are made using "curly flex" (BX) cables or Adaptaflex lines.

A simple, temporary link between the new hall and the social club is a semicircular tube 82'/25 m long and 15'/4.5 m wide, made from curved corrugated steel sheets on lightweight steel frames with a continuous translucent blue skylight. The link provides storage space for the heavy sports apparatus and contains the main electrical distribution board.

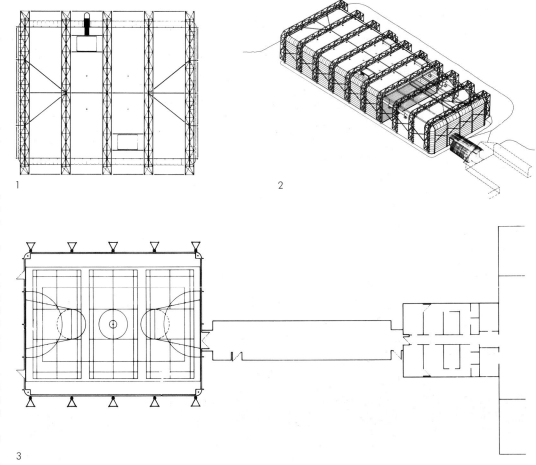

1

2

3

4

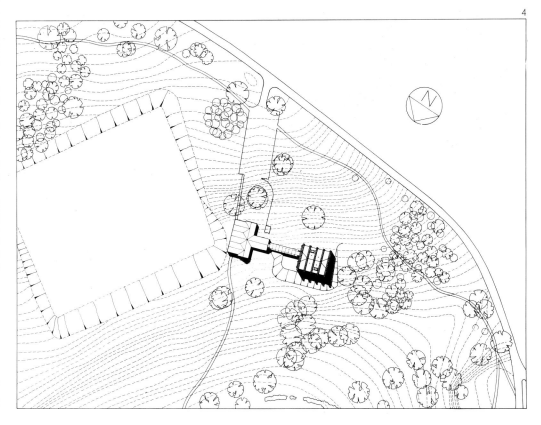

5

6

1. Roof plan showing external structure.

2. Isometric view, including possible future extension.

3. Plan.

4. Site plan.

5. The sports hall in its mature parkland setting.

6. Curved corner panels are translucent.

7

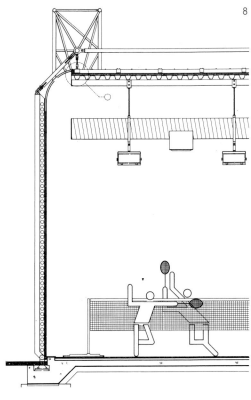

8

9

10

7. The external structure leaves the interior almost completely free of obstructions.

8. Detail section.

9., 10. A very elaborate and decorative structure supports a very simple enclosing envelope.

Ice Rink, Oxford
Architects: Nicholas Grimshaw and Partners
Completed 1984

The main requirements were that this project be self-financing as far as possible in both capital and running costs, that it be a high-quality building, and that it be open in time for the 1984/85 winter season. The two main design problems were to provide an economical technical solution for a highly specialized building type and to create an exciting image that would attract the public in large numbers. The architect's solution was to enclose all the ice rink facilities in one simple envelope and rely on the structure of the building to create the image.

There were two powerful influences on the structural solution: the ground conditions, which implied the need for piling; and the requirement for a wide span over the ice pad. Most of the roof loads are picked up by a spine beam and transmitted by means of stainless steel tension rods to a mast at each end of the building. Each mast is founded on a group of four piles and stabilized by being anchored to the edge beam of the building and to a group of four tension piles. Thus there is a total of only sixteen piles. Cladding loads rest on simple strip foundations around the perimeter. All the suspension elements of the structure are in stainless steel, which should need no maintenance. Only the masts themselves will need to be painted at intervals of about ten years. There are only four roof penetrations, and they have been carefully detailed and insulated.

Access to the building is at first floor level via a gentle ramp from Oxpens Road. Management and reception functions are on the first floor with the bar, function room, and shop. This means that the service facilities, which are of an equivalent area, can be at rink level. These include the plant room, boot hire, main toilets, cafeteria, and sweet shop. Boot changing is around the rink, on "tractor seats".

Large numbers of fixed tiered seats would have conflicted with the requirement for people to circulate freely around the rink in close contact with the ice, so pull-out "bleacher" seating has been provided for the relatively infrequent ice hockey matches. The ice is visible from the first floor reception gallery, from the two long galleries on each side of the rink, and from the raised seating areas of the bar. The glass north end of the building allows passersby in Oxpens Road to see the skaters, and gives the skaters a sense of contact with the outside world. This glazing is particularly effective at night.

The intention is that the ice rink will form the first element in a large leisure complex. The next element will be a swimming pool created by extending the spine beam and adding two further masts. The bar/restaurant and management offices at the south end of the ice rink will be enlarged and re-orientated so as to form a central core serving in two directions.

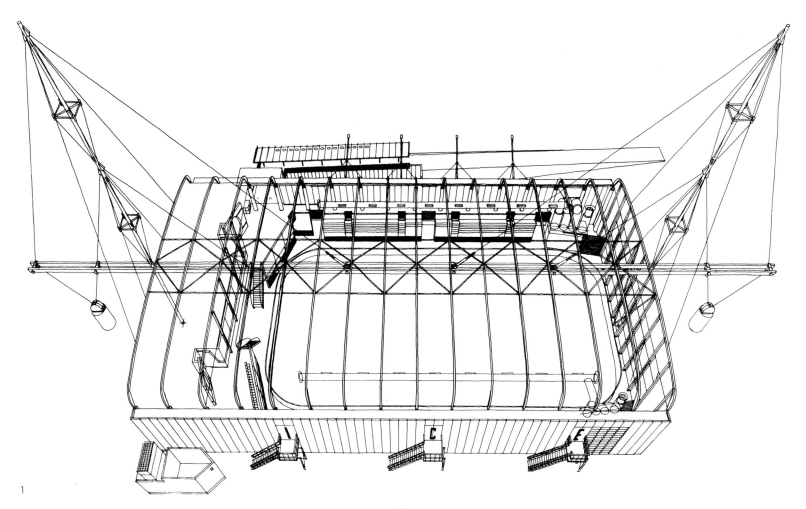

1

1. Perspective showing clearly the principles of the structure. The roof membrane is pierced at only four points.

2. Section through entrance ramp and bleacher seating.

3. First floor and ground floor plans. The main entrance is at first floor level.
Key: 1 main entrance, 2 bleacher seating, 3 bar, 4 conference room, 5 café, 6 skate hire, 7 ice plant, 8 changing rooms.

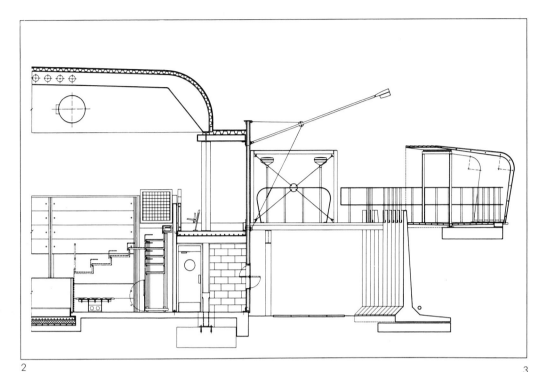

2

3

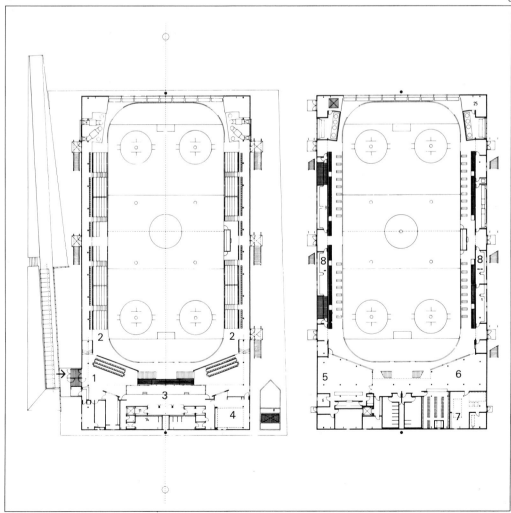

4. The interior is industrial in character, as are many High Tech leisure buildings.

5. Twin nautical staircases from main entrance to ice level.

6. A two-masted schooner, complete with bowsprit.

Office and Workshop for Ladkarn Ltd, London
Architects: Nicholas Grimshaw and Partners
Completed 1985

Ladkarn (Haulage) Ltd are groundwork contractors who were originally based in Bermondsey. When they decided to move to larger, custom-built premises, they investigated a number of sites in the London Docklands Enterprise Zone and were eventually offered a prominent 1.1 acre site in the north east corner of West India Dock.

The programme was for 9,680 sq.ft./900 m² of vehicle maintenance workshop, with a clear headroom of 21'/6.5 m, and 7,000 sq.ft./650 m² of offices. An important requirement was for the workshop to be column-free, since vehicles of the size and weight that were normally serviced could cause considerable structural damage even when moving at slow speeds. External parking for 14 trucks and 18 cars was also required.

The office block at the front of the building is of orthodox steel frame construction and is protected from the workshop area by a 4-hour fire wall. Executive offices are on the second upper floor and have direct access to a roof terrace, which affords spectacular views over the docks.

It is the external steel structure of the maintenance workshop – a mast and stay system transferring forces over and around the offices – that distinguishes the building. As well as providing the column-free workshop space and easing the foundation problems along the dock edge, the exposed structure signals the presence of the building in an unmistakable fashion. Circular hollow-steel sections and Macalloy tie bars form a structure that is legible both in concept and detail. The nautical flavour is deliberate. The main horizontal spars were pre-stressed in the fabricator's works so that all bars, including those to resist wind uplift, remain taut under normal conditions.

The external truck parking area is screened from the adjoining sites by a curved fence clad in the same horizontal profiled metal as the building.

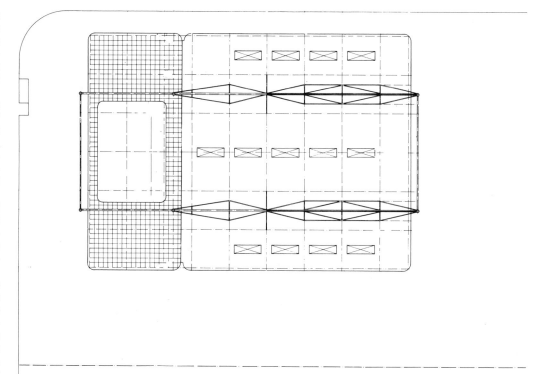

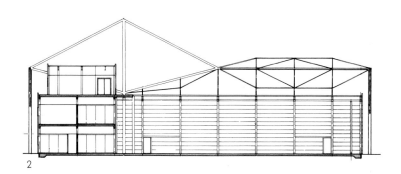

2

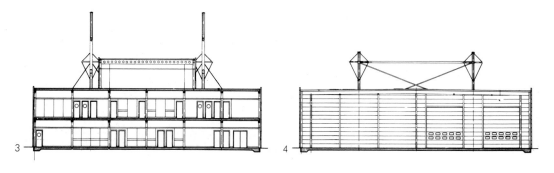

3   4

1. Roof plan.

2. Section with offices on the left, maintenance workshop on the right.

3. Section through offices.

4. Elevation of workshop.

5. Elaborate external structure, painted High Tech red.

6. Building and sailing barge: complementary images.

5

6

**Architect's own house and studio, Downshire Hill,
Hampstead, London
Architects: Michael Hopkins and Partners
Completed 1976**

The house is sited in a conservation area. The design tries to achieve as much as possible with the minimum of structure. Construction techniques developed for larger buildings have been adapted for use on a domestic scale. The plan is very simple: two rectangular floors linked by a central spiral staircase with no permanent partitioning except to bathrooms and storage. The street and garden elevations are fully glazed and the street entrance is at upper floor level.

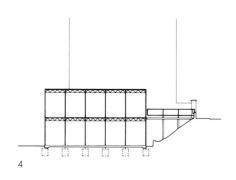

1

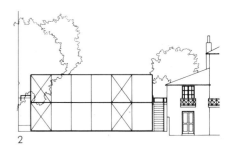

2

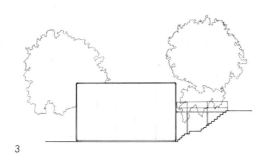

3

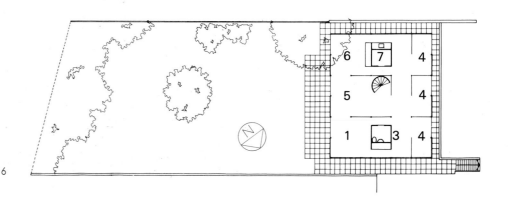

4

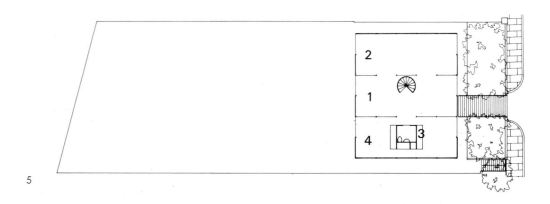

5

1. Elevation from street.

2. Elevation from garden.

3. Side elevation.

4. Section showing entrance bridge.

5. Upper floor plan.

6. Ground floor plan.
Key: 1 sitting, 2 studio, 3 shower room,
4 sleeping, 5 dining, 6 cooking, 7 storage.

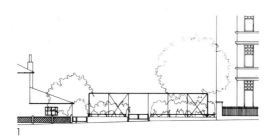

6

100

7. Street front.

8. Garden front.

9. Ground floor interior showing steel lattice beams.

10. Finishes are a mixture of industrial and domestic materials.

11. Steel spiral staircase.

8

7

9

10

11

**Draught Beer Department, Greene King Brewery,
Bury St Edmunds, Suffolk
Architects: Michael Hopkins and Partners
Completed 1979**

This is a 35,000 sq.ft./3,250 m² highly serviced process plant and storage building. It includes cask cleaning and filling facilities, rest rooms for staff, and beer truck loading bays. The design reflects the sequence of production and allows expansion by a further 18,000 sq.ft./1,670 m². The building stands in the flood plain of the River Linnett, so the floor slab is raised above ground. This corresponds to the loading dock height for beer trucks.

1

2

1. Loading bay. The building is raised off the ground like a piece of machinery.

2. Glazed roller shutters.

102

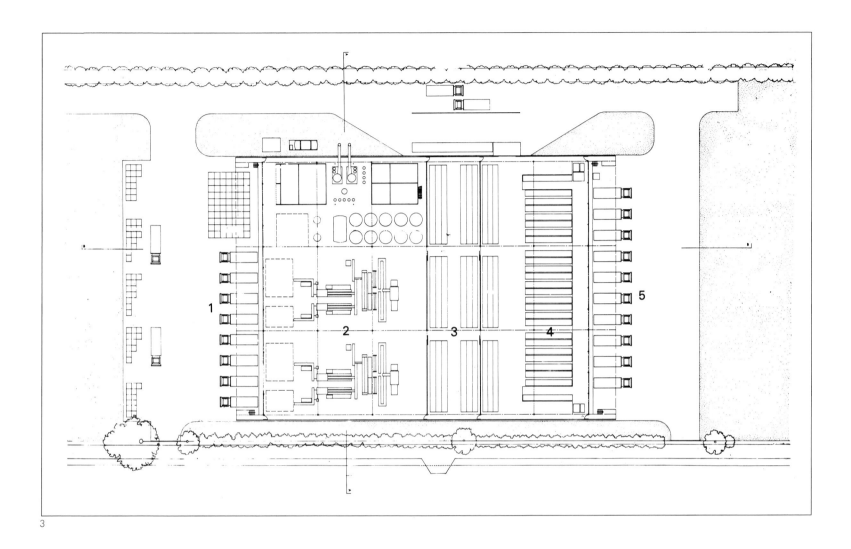

3. Plan.
Key: 1 unloading bays, 2 washing and racking,
3 cooled full store, 4 pantry, 5 loading bays.

4. Perspective section.

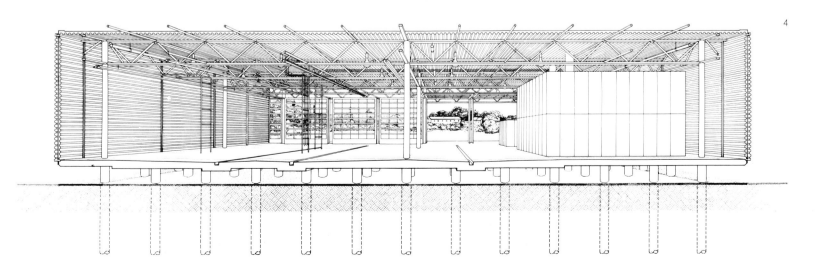

4

"Patera" Nursery Industrial Units
Architects: Michael Hopkins and Partners
System designed 1981

The Patera Building System was developed in response to the demand for high quality standard buildings that could be used as nursery industrial units, research laboratories, or offices. The system can produce very flexible enclosures of various sizes. A complete structure and envelope package is provided so that all building regulations requirements are solved at the source. The buildings are quick to erect on a prepared concrete slab. New structural and cladding systems were developed to fulfil these requirements. Cladding panels are supported by external, parallel-welded tubular-steel, portal-frame trusses linked by stainless steel connectors to hollow-section purlins and angle cross rails. The external structural frame acts with the cladding panels to minimize the need for additional wind bracing. The cladding provides structural bracing, weather protection, thermal insulation and fire protection. The panels are self-finished inside and out so that no internal lining is required. Each panel is sealed with its own ethylene-propylene gasket.

Michael Hopkins and Partners' own office in Marylebone, London, was built using Patera construction techniques. The 4,300 sq.ft./400 m² building has an open plan, with a mezzanine floor and a double height space.

1

2

1. The Hopkins office in Marylebone is an adaptation of the Patera building system.

2. Office interior with steel spiral stair.

3

4

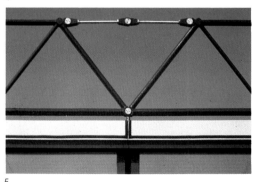

5

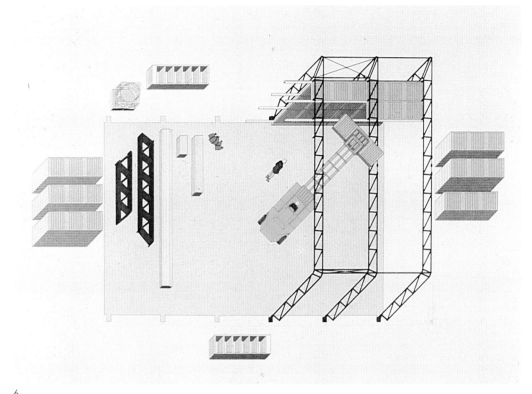

6

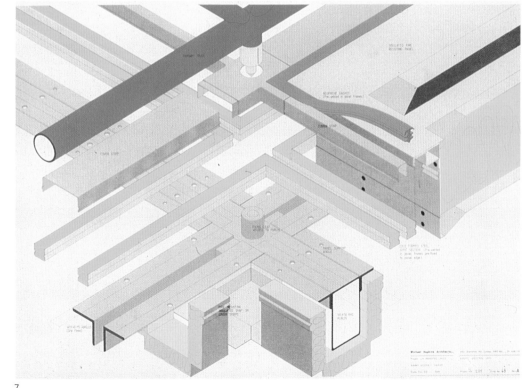

7

3.–5. The external structure is a lattice portal frame of extreme slenderness.

6. Diagram of construction sequence.

7. External walls and roof use the same Neoprene gasket-sealed panel system.

Enclosure of Shopping Centre, Basildon, Essex
Architects: Michael Hopkins and Partners
Project. Design completed 1987

The programme was to design an enclosure for the Town Square shopping centre to enable it to compete with other nearby retail developments. The intention was to provide protection from the weather, to improve the environment by upgrading finishes and to reinforce the Town Square as the focus for surrounding communities.

The enclosure has a 100,000 sq.ft./9,300 m² roof of transparent Teflon membrane suspended and tensioned by a centrally supported, light steel structure. The membrane oversails and is sealed against the buildings. It has good fire retarding, light transmission, and thermal properties, and it allows plant growth below. The project is financed by the provision of 70,000 sq.ft./6,500 m² of new retail floor area on two levels in the centre of the square. The existing shops will remain open during construction.

A satisfactory passive-thermal performance is achieved with temperatures 5 to 6 degrees warmer than outside in winter. Natural ventilation and fire ventilation are also achieved by passive means. Low-level inlets are combined with linear smoke louvres at the high points of the structural bays.

There will be additional attractions such as a chair-plane ride, luxuriant planting, and talking newspapers.

1

1. Model showing how the new structure covers the pedestrian precinct between existing buildings.

2. Ring around mast, clamping and tensioning the glass fibre membrane.

3. New shops in the middle of the pedestrian precinct.

2

3

**Abbey Hill Golf Club, Milton Keynes,
Buckinghamshire
Architects: Michael Hopkins and Partners
Completed 1982**

The building is a golf club and pub, with changing rooms, a professional shop, licensee's accommodation, bars, and an external terrace. It is sited in the centre of and overlooking the golf course. A translucent membrane solar shading device is cantilevered from armatures on all sides of the building.

2

3

1

1. Membrane awnings reflected in the glass curtain wall.

2. External bar terrace.

3. Membrane awning, showing tensioning device.

Research Laboratories for Schlumberger, Cambridge, Great Britain
**Architects: Michael Hopkins and Partners
Completed 1984**

The client required a centre for research into aspects of oil exploration, including drilling and fluid mechanics, rock and wellbore physics, and computer modelling of drilling information. The programme stressed the need for contact between scientists of different departments. Facilities for meetings with university personnel and staff from other companies were also required. The building was to be capable of 50% expansion.

The design provides as many contact points as possible between areas for theoretical and experimental research, administrators and researchers, recreation and work, large- and small-scale activities, and the inside and outside. The concept is simple: two single-storey research wings running north/south, separated by 79'/24 m wide covered spaces — the test station and the winter garden — housing large-scale activities. The ends of the research wings are left open for future expansion.

The superstructure is a steel frame in which two different systems are overlaid on each other, one for the large spans of the test station and winter garden, the other for the short spans of the research wings. The central areas are covered with a translucent Teflon-coated glass fibre membrane. This long-spanning tensile material held in double curvature throughout its surface admits natural light to the centre of the deep plan.

The research wings are fully glazed on both internal and external faces with polyester-coated aluminium-framed sliding doors. Flat roofs are covered with a single-layer polymeric membrane on a profiled steel deck. Floors are of suspended construction, spanning the service zones below. Air handling units draw fresh air under the building and serve the sealed, air-conditioned internal laboratories.

In the test station are three drilling test pits up to 65'/20 m deep, and an underground high-pressure pump chamber. The activities in this space are acoustically separated from surrounding areas by 7/8"/21 mm thick laminated glass. Services in the test station run under a raised grating floor for greater flexibility. A 10-ton gantry crane covers the entire floor area, with a maximum hook height of 33'/10 m. Specialist services are located in external compounds and fed into the building by pipes running behind embankments.

continued on page 110 ▶

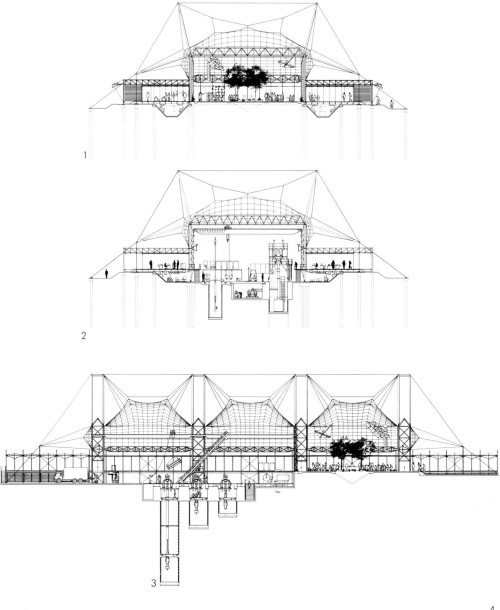

1

2

3

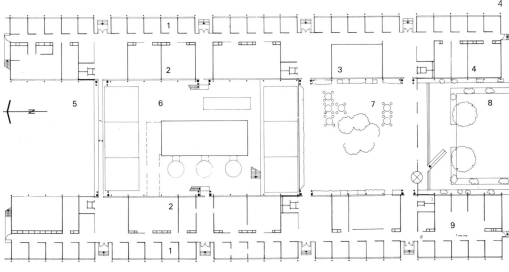

4

1. Cross section through winter garden.

2. Cross section through test station.

3. Longitudinal section.

4. Plan.
Key: 1 scientists' offices, 2 laboratories, 3 kitchen, 4 computer, 5 service yard, 6 drilling test station, 7 restaurant, 8 terrace, 9 secretaries.

5. Linear buildings are simple, Miesian structures, somewhat similar to the Patera buildings (p. 104).

6. Teflon-coated glass fibre membrane being hoisted into position.

7. Linear buildings under construction.

5

6

7

Research Laboratories for Schlumberger,
Cambridge, Great Britain

Internal partitions are demountable PVC-faced chipboard panels that also form a storage wall system. Corridor walls are 50% glazed and doors are plate glass. Ceilings are acoustic metal tiles. The only service at high level is lighting; all others are fed from the floor. Thermal insulation has been concentrated where it is most effective, in the roofs and floors of the research wings. The deep plan means that central areas receive heat from surrounding laboratories and become tempered buffer zones.

8

9

10

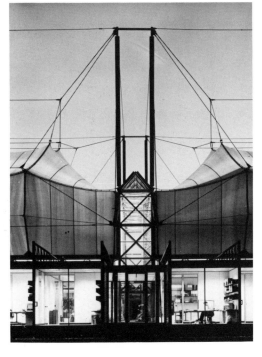

8. Inside the tent: winter garden and restaurant.

9. Perimeter offices are completely glazed.

10. The membrane itself is not characteristically High Tech, but the external suspension structure is.

11. The two types of structure — flat-roofed linear blocks and membrane enclosures — are separate but overlapping.

Cummins Engine Company Ltd, Shotts, Lanarkshire
Architects: Ahrends, Burton and Koralek
Completed 1983

The redevelopment took place around and among factory buildings in which Cummins operated for the previous 25 years. The new factory has the capacity to produce 90 250–400 horsepower diesel engines a day. The production space is divided into four areas: receiving, machining, stores and assembly, and testing and shipping. The plan allows for future expansion of up to 30%.

Above the east/west production flow there is a separate north/south pedestrian circulation system connecting to the car park at a higher level of the site. The car park stretches the full length of the factory, allowing people to park near their place of work. Three covered bridges provide direct access into the factory at the upper level, clear of materials movement.

New production areas of the buildings are structured on a 49.2'/15 m square grid. Pin-jointed tubular-steel columns support welded tubular-steel primary trusses. Reinforced concrete stub columns at low level protect against impact by forklift trucks. The secondary roof structure takes the form of castellated steel joists fixed below the bottom members of the primary trusses. Steel rod hangers connect the primary trusses and castellated beams at 1/3 intervals across the 49.2'/15 m span. The roof profile follows this geometric configuration and provides a continuous zone for

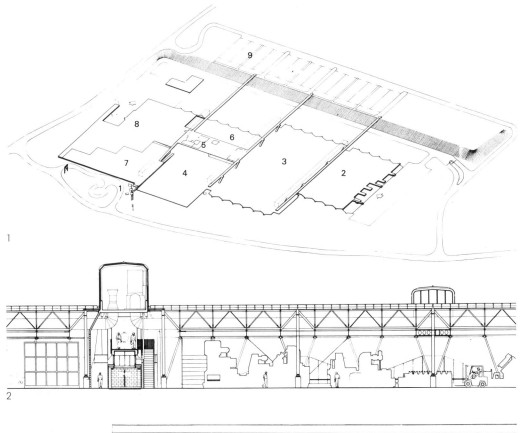

1

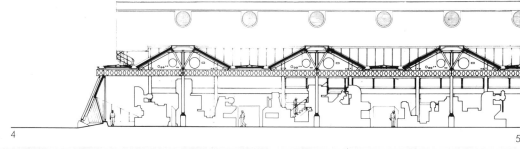

2

4

5

3

distribution of primary services. Secondary services are distributed within the depth of the secondary structure.

Zones between adjacent production areas are structured by reinforced concrete frames supporting the first floor walkways and roof-level plant rooms.

Cladding for roof and walls consists of an inner skin of corrugated structural steel decking, steel spacer purlins, and mill-finished corrugated aluminium sheeting externally. Cavities are filled with insulation.

6

7

1. Isometric showing general arrangement of the plan.
Key: 1 main entrance, 2 receiving, 3 machining, 4 main stores, 5 canteen, 6 assembly, 7 offices, 8 final assembly, 9 car park.

2. Section through raised walkway.

3. Detail at perimeter of production area.

4. Section through production area.

5. Car park and pedestrian access bridges are visible on the right.

6. High-level plant enclosure hovering over the main structure.

7. The complex geometry at the perimeter is typical of this architectural practice rather than of High Tech in general.

**Supermarket for J Sainsbury, Canterbury, Kent
Architects: Ahrends, Burton and Koralek
Completed 1984**

The design was the winning entry in a limited competition promoted by Sainsbury's in 1982.

The site lies to the east of Canterbury, with open views of the city dominated by the cathedral. The building consists of three linked clear-span spaces for sales, storage and preparation, and goods receiving. Flat roofs are supported on slender steel beams suspended from tubular steel masts by stayed tie rods. The silver-coloured masts and ties give height and vertical emphasis to an otherwise low-lying building on a rather featureless site, and provide a visual echo of the tower and pinnacles of the distant cathedral.

The shop front, which faces onto a large car park, is clad in square aluminium and glass panels. A Teflon-coated glass fibre canopy is suspended from the main masts along the length of the shop front terminating in a quarter circle at the entrance lobby, which is supported from a central mast giving visual emphasis to the main entrance.

The superstructure is of two distinct types. The main type is a clear-span suspended steel structure that covers the sales area (9 bays of 23' x 118'/7 x 36 m), the bulk stock area (6 bays of 23' x 75'/7 x 23 m) and the unloading area (3 bays of 23' x 75'/7 x 23 m). This structure is designed to provide large spaces free of columns. Dropped roofs 16.4'/5 m wide separate these three areas and house the main plant. The secondary type of superstructure, for the staff accommodation and plant room, is a conventional steel frame.

The main column masts are twin 8.6"/245 mm diameter tubes with welded stiffener/connection plates. The bottoms of the masts are grouted into pockets in the pilecaps with a high strength, non-shrinking grout. The main rafters are 12"/350 mm universal beams. They are supported from the tops of the twin column masts

continued on page 116 ▶

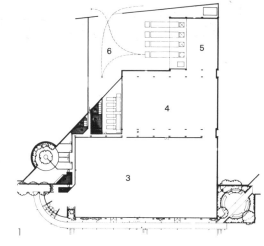

1

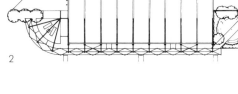

2

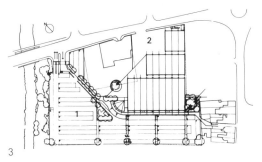

3

4

1. Plan.

2. Roof plan.

3. Site plan.
Key: 1 car park, 2 vehicle yard, 3 sales area, 4 storage and preparation, 5 unloading bay, 6 vehicle yard.

4. Isometric showing structural system.

5. The masts are highly finished and beautifully proportioned.

6. The canopy over the external walkway is suspended from the masts.

5

7

at the 1/3 points on the 118'/36 m span and at the mid-points on the 75'/23 m span. The suspension system consists of twin 2"/60 mm diameter solid rods with turnbuckles for adjustment. Castings are welded to the rod ends and connected to the plates attached to the columns and rafters by 2.6"/75 mm diameter steel pins.

The roof is of metal deck construction, with insulation and high-performance felt finish, supported on steel purlins at 5'9"/1.75 m centres spanning between the main rafters. The entire roof construction is contained within the main rafter depth, resulting in a total roof thickness of only 14"/400 mm. All steelwork was grit-blasted at the works. The surface treatment is a silver polyurethane paint to a high specification.

Because of the lateral movement of the main suspended structure, the external walls, of glass block and aluminium curtain wall construction, are supported by freestanding reinforced concrete columns with movement joints at the roof/wall junctions.

8

7. Curved wall at the main entrance.

8. Supermarket and cathedral. The masts have been
compared to Gothic buttresses and finials.

Doughnut House
Architects: Future Systems
Project, 1986

Low profile earthshielded houses have great potential at a time when conservation issues are increasingly important. This house is sunk into the landcape to avoid conflict in culturally or historically sensitive settings. Earth-shielded homes are highly energy efficient and help to preserve the local ecology by minimizing the impact on the natural environment and topology. The Doughnut House can be built on various slopes with various depths of earth shielding. The basic structure is a stressed skin circular torus with an open central courtyard. Access is by a short tunnel connected to the outer perimeter. The central courtyard is landscaped and combines complete privacy with ample daylighting of all internal areas through the sloping glazed inner wall. Upward-lifting doors provide access to the courtyard. Two equipment options can be used to control and condition daylight – a revolving louvred frame around the courtyard edge to shade south-facing rooms, and a pivoted mirror to reflect sunlight into north-facing rooms.

The main materials are aluminium or GRP for the structural shell segments and glazing frames. A variety of soft finishes are used for internal walls and furniture.

1. Plan and horizontal section through retaining wall.

2. Isometric. Note entrance hatch, sun reflector, antenna and satellite dish. High Tech architects delight in add-on technical gadgets.

3. Construction sequence and cross section, showing relationship between living spaces and central courtyard.

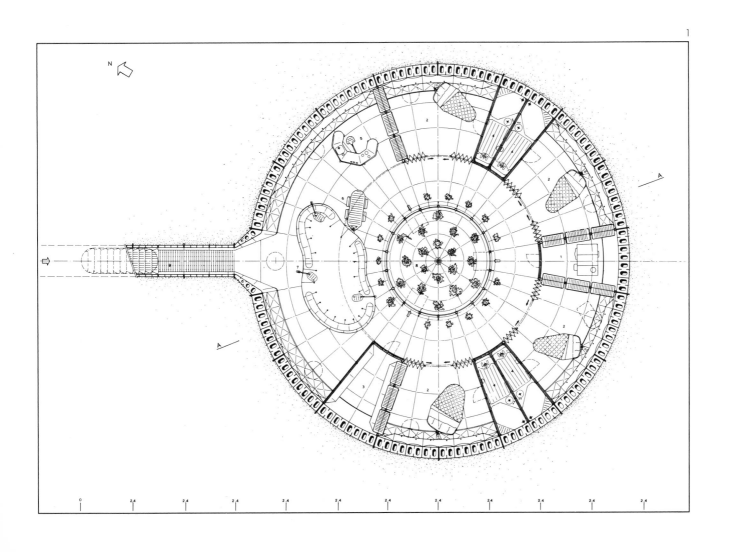

1

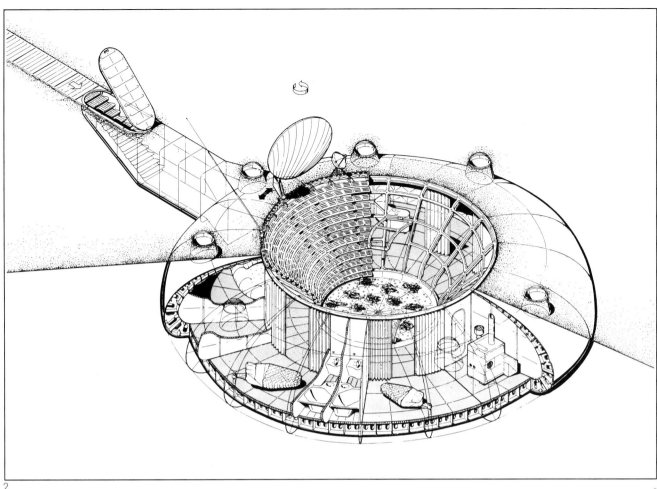

2

3

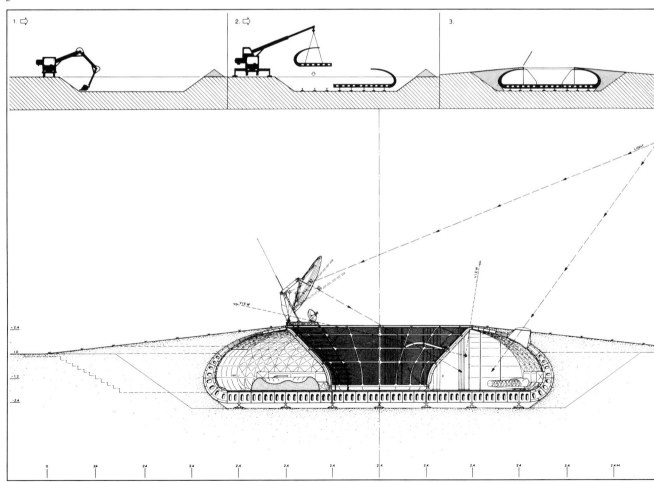

Harrods "Way in" Shop, London
Architects: Future Systems and Jiricna, Kerr
Associates
Completed 1985

The programme was for refurbishing part of the fourth floor at Harrods department store to accommodate fashions, hairdressing, restaurant, studio and offices. The total area is approximately 37,600 sq.ft./3,500 m². Perimeter walls, assembled from vacuum-formed aluminium panels and standing frames, divide the display areas from the changing and stock rooms. The walls can be rearranged to enable these areas to grow and shrink. Existing walls and ceiling are matt black to heighten the visual impact of the mobile display elements. An aluminium, tubular suspended ceiling has been introduced over certain key areas. The floor is reconstituted black granite for maximum durability.

There are more than 150 custom-designed mobile aluminium units for the display of merchandise; units incorporate interchangeable shelves, hanging rails, mirrors and display tables. Each display unit is equipped with low-voltage lighting and a dished reflector. The units are spray-finished with silver metallic paint. The design team was also responsible for the new shop logo, shopping bags, restaurant menu, cosmetics packaging, clothes hangers and photographic wall murals.

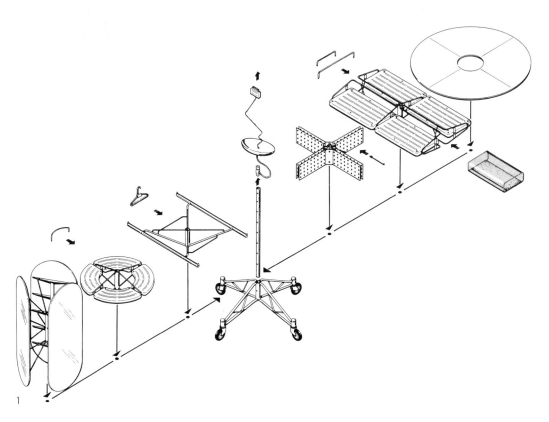

1. Mobile display module unit with optional fittings.

2. The fittings in action.

3. Note the low-voltage light in the top of the column with a convex reflector above.

4. The suspended ceiling is made from extruded aluminium tubes.

5. Axonometric of whole department.

3

4

5

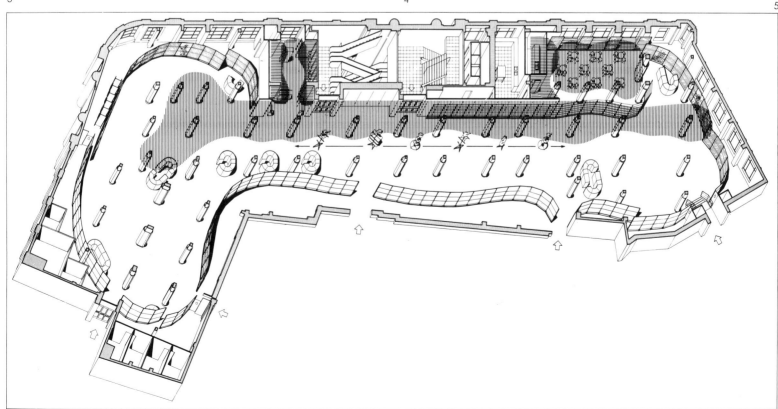

Computer Centre, Lennox Wood
Architects: Michael Aukett Associates
Completed 1985

This high-security computer headquarters is set in a 60-acre park shaped from a derelict brickworks. Views over the newly created parkland and lakes were a major consideration in the selection of the site and in the orientation and arrangement of the building. The dramatic setting required a building in sympathy with its surroundings; the programme, however, required a high level of security. From this conflict emerged the concept of a pavilion set on a plateau above a stone wall forming a ha-ha wall to conceal the security fencing.

The building encloses 92,000 sq.ft./8,550 m² of floor space with a 10,000 sq.ft./929 m² computer machine hall. Ancillary office accommodation is arranged around the secure computer machine hall and overlooks the country park and lakes. The deep plan office space is naturally lit by a continuous lantern over a main circulation street through the middle of the building. A system of slats filters light through the lantern.

The floors within the building are supported on table columns. The truss roof spans between external tubular columns that also support an external *brise-soleil*. This is designed to reduce solar heat gain and minimize sky glare during the summer, which would otherwise pose serious problems for the many users of computer VDUs in the building. It also provides a continuous window-cleaning gantry. Aluminium-framed solar glass panels form the external skin of the building.

The computer machine hall is serviced from an undercroft that allows free planning of the machines in the hall. Only three columns support the structure above. The engineering plant provides heat recovery from the machine hall to the offices, and electricity generation in the event of mains power failure. Floors are raised throughout the building.

Simple high-quality materials are intended to reflect the image of an established company operating in the forefront of computer technology.

1

1. The site is part of reclaimed brickworks.

2., 3. The *brises-soleil* reduce heat gain and minimize sky glare.

4. External columns support roof trusses and *brises-soleil.*

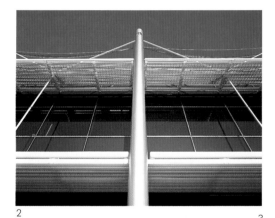

2

3

4

House, Woodgreen, Hampshire
Architect: Richard Horden
Completed 1984

A concrete base supports a "wind frame" assembled from oval-section aluminium tubes made by a manufacturer of yacht masts. Columns on a 11.8"/8.6 m square grid are linked by spars and given lateral stability by tension cables. The connections are stainless steel crosses that slide into the tubes and are fixed with bolts and sleeves. The frame acts as a services-distribution network and is infilled in a variety of ways. Roof panels of metal decking, insulation and an aluminium-faced bituthene waterproof membrane have steel angle frames to transfer loads directly to the columns. External walls are either aluminium weatherboarding or full-height, full-width, glazed sliding doors. Ceilings are white aluminium clip-on slats. Two bays of the wind frame are left open and fitted with screening devices, such as corrugated aluminium canopies, trellises, louvres, and retractable "sail" awnings.

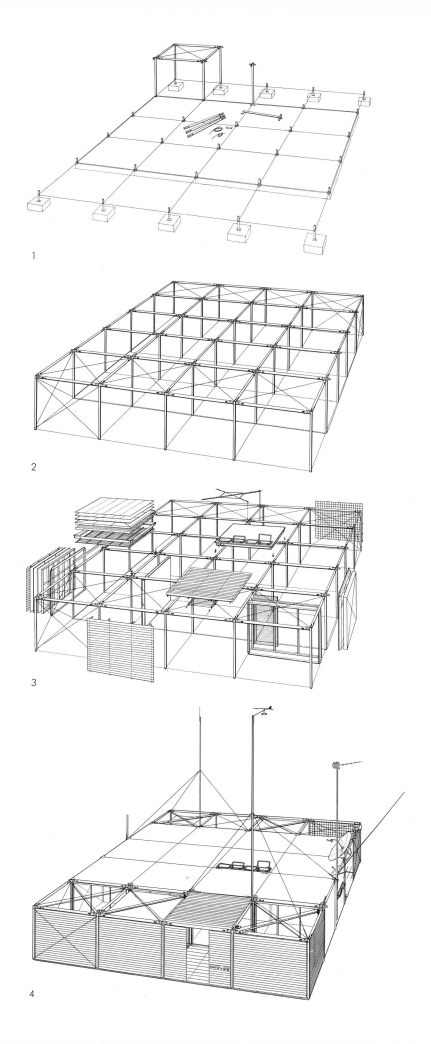

1

2

3

1.–4. Construction sequence from concrete slab to satellite dish: the familiar High Tech kit of parts philosophy, in this case nautical parts.

4

124

5

6

5. The "wind frame" encloses external as well as internal spaces.

6. Oval section members were made by a manufacturer of yacht masts.

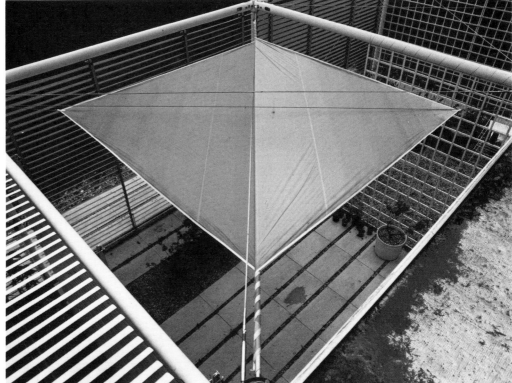

7. Lateral stability of the frame is achieved by tension cables.

8. Ceilings are white aluminium clip-on slats.

9. Sail/sun-shade.

Eagle Rock House, Crowborough, Sussex
Architect: Ian Ritchie
Completed 1980

The client's wish for the form of a bird is translated through the articulated structure and the suspension of the wings. The tail is a trapped crystal greenhouse, its protected plants a counterpoint to the natural landscape of oaks, holly, and sandstone. The movement of the external blinds is a play on the ruffling of the bird's feathers in response to the climate. The loft space (the bird's head) is the focus and energy centre of the house.

The structure centres on an inclined A frame of circular hollow-steel sections that provides a core for the suspension of the body of the building and its two wings. The body is constructed of Vierendeel trusses supported by goalpost frames that also provide lateral stability. At the main entrance, the ends of the Vierendeel trusses are suspended from the A frame. The wings are prismatic trusses supported by the body and by suspension rods from the central A frame. Small A frames at the ends provide lateral stability.

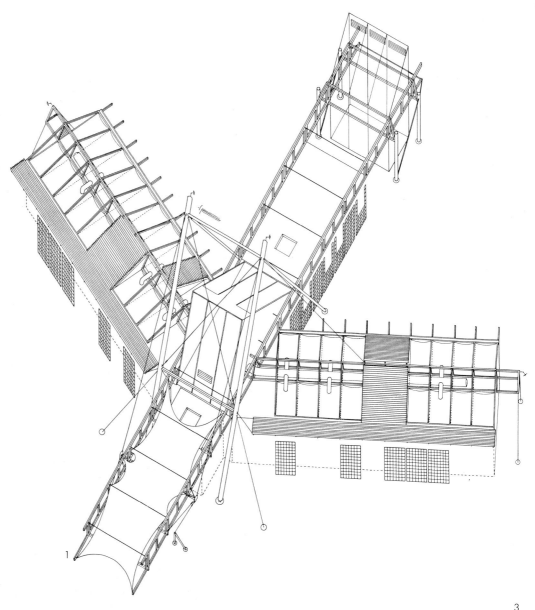

1

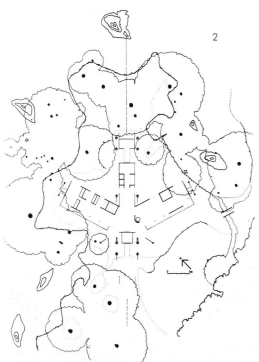

2

3

1. Axonometric. Fuselage and wings, more like an aeroplane than a bird.

2. Site plan.

3. External blinds move, says the architect, like ruffled feathers.

4., 5. The site is a secluded grove of oak and holly.

6. Entrance canopy has a membrane roof.

6

4

5

Link Centre, Swindon, Wiltshire
Architects: Thamesdown Borough Council
Architects
Completed 1985

The Link Centre provides for community, arts, and sports activities in one building. The accommodation includes a district library, offices, an ice rink, a multi-purpose sports hall, a swimming pool, squash courts, a snooker parlour, a health and fitness suite, a studio theatre, and a large community hall. The building is the focal point for a developing community of 50,000 people in west Swindon.

A short design and construction period was necessary to minimize devaluation of a fixed end-cost figure. This determined the construction method and the selection of materials. A single-roof umbrella was constructed to allow the design of the interior to develop free of constraint from supporting columns. This roof and the profiled steel cladding also provided shelter for the construction of the interior. The internal structure is a steel frame with precast concrete flooring and block-work partitions. Services are exposed for easy access and maintenance.

Heat recovery from recirculated air and a highly insulated external envelope help to minimize energy demand. Waste heat from the rink refrigeration provides for most of the heating needs of the complex.

1

2

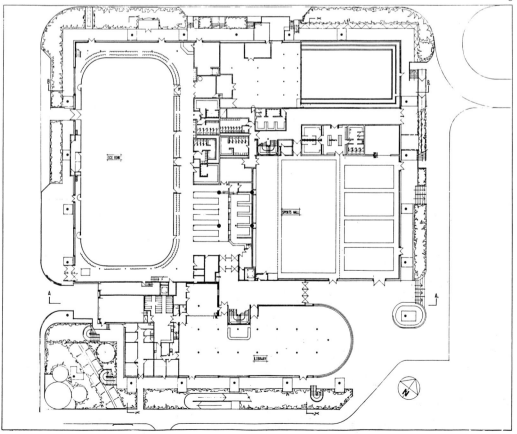

3

1. The single-roof umbrella allowed the design of the interior to proceed independently.

2. Entrance ramp on the south side of the building.

3. Ground floor plan.

4. Ductwork is exposed internally in the approved High Tech manner.

5. Unusually, the structure is painted white, leaving the primary colours for other elements.

4

5

Medical Faculty, Technical University of Aachen, West Germany
Architects: Weber, Brand and Partners
Completed 1984

The building, or megastructure, contains lecture theatres, laboratories, cafeterias and other teaching, research, and social facilities, as well as wards, and diagnostic and treatment facilities. 24 towers, 177'/ 54 m tall, in four rows of six, dominate the composition. These house the vertical circulation and plant. The main structure, of in situ and precast concrete, is animated visually by yellow and silver external steel ducts and by red painted steel cradles, railings, stairs, and canopies. Inside, the metal detailing and strong colours draw attention away from the massive concrete structure.

Most of the accommodation is in areas that span between, and are serviced from, parallel bands of structure. There are also large landscaped courtyards. Circulation routes within the building are organized to encourage casual social and educational encounters. Access is from parking stretched adjacent to the long southern edge of the building. Beyond the entrance foyer are lecture theatres, library, restaurant, cafeteria, and seminar rooms. On the next two floors are the various medical departments with their consulting rooms and treatment facilities. The wards are in narrower wings on the top three floors and look into the courtyards, some of which open only through these top three floors. Others open right down to the entrance floor. Below the entrance floor is another level of storerooms and services.

1. 24 towers dominate the composition.

2. Perspective section, showing towers, courtyards, and roof gardens.

3. Detail, elevation of tower.

1

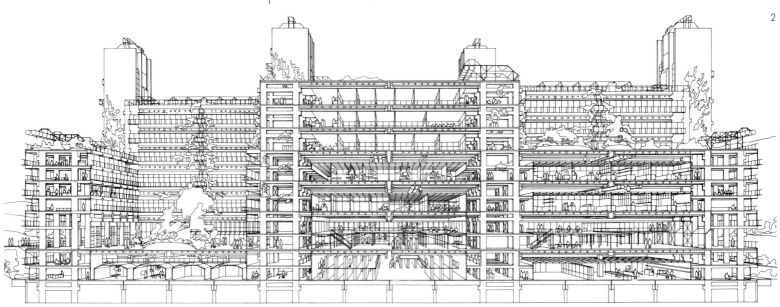

2

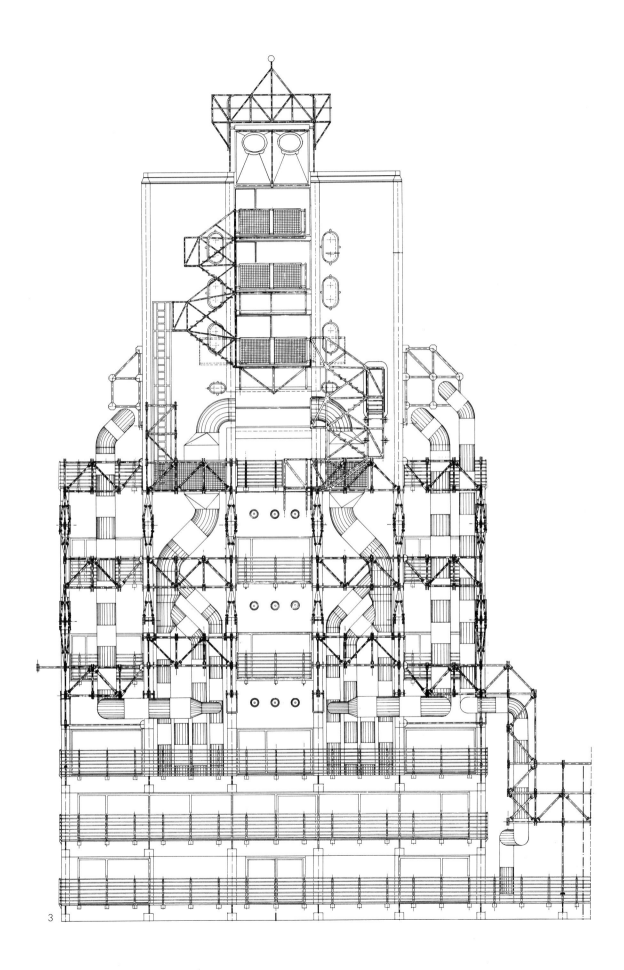

3

Medical Faculty, Technical University of Aachen,
West Germany

4. As an object in the landscape, it is more like a power station than a hospital.

5. Ground floor plan.

6. Courtyards and roof gardens punctuate the building.

4

5

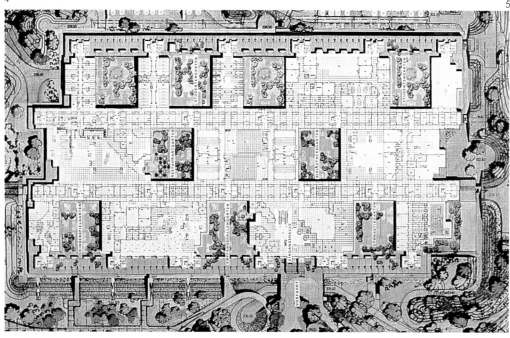

7

8

7. Exterior steel railings, canopies, and staircases are all painted red.

8. Most of the internal components are of metal, but the main structure is reinforced concrete.

9. Lurid green carpet dominates the public spaces.

10. Vehicle-like information desk.

9

10

Medical Faculty, Technical University of Aachen,
West Germany

11. The towers house vertical circulation and plant.

12. External detailing is very complex and occasionally riotous.

13. Though not completed until 1984, the design of this building actually precedes that of the Centre Pompidou.

11

12

Schulitz House, Beverly Hills, California
Architect: Helmut Schulitz
Completed 1976

The house is designed to answer the needs of a 4-person family. It emphasizes the use of communal areas for family, friends and guests, rather than private spaces for individuals. It responds sensitively to a difficult but spectacular site and takes advantage of a magnificent view towards the city and the ocean. It also provides outdoor spaces which the steep slope naturally denies.

The steel structure was erected by crane in two days, creating horizontal decks from which work could proceed safely. Wherever possible connections were bolted rather than welded. The frame structure allows all walls to be non-loadbearing and demountable.

Adjustable louvres protect the outdoor deck and the glass on the main level against heat gain. There is no air conditioning. Natural cross-ventilation, with the heat rising and escaping through the upper level windows, is sufficient even in the hot summer months. The heating is a conventional forced air system with registers at the perimeter of the building on the lower two floors.

The house is an experimental building for an open system building method making maximum use of pre-finished industrial components straight from manufacturers' catalogues.

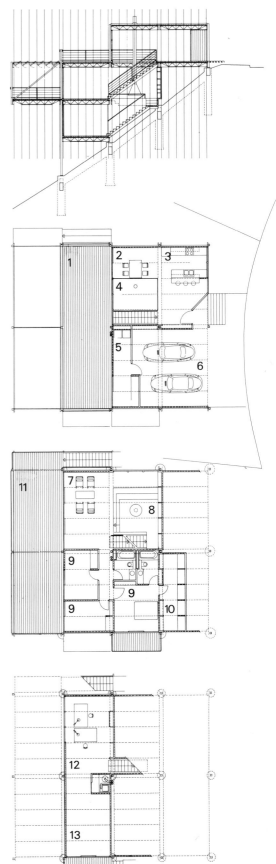

1. High Tech houses work well when the architect is also the client.

2. Foor plans and section showing steeply sloping site.
Key: 1 sun deck, 2 dining, 3 kitchen, 4 void, 5 wash, 6 car port, 7 living, 8 conversation pit, 9 bedroom, 10 store, 11 covered deck, 12 studio, 13 playroom.

3. Cantilevered terrace with magnificent views to the city and the ocean.

4. Steel frame is exposed externally, with prominence given to diagonal bracing.

2

3

4

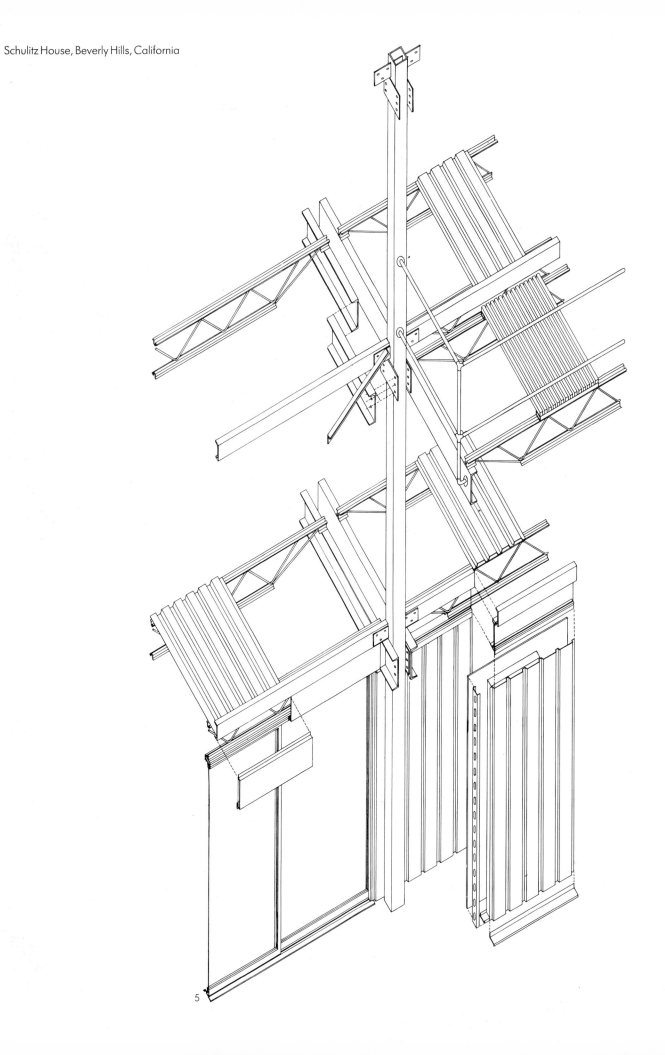

5

6

7

5. Axonometric showing construction from simple off-the-shelf components.

6. Obligatory primary colours, including small touches of red.

7. Detailing is direct and austere, rather than refined.

8

8. High Tech hearth.

9. Lattice trusses and metal decking, undisguised in
the interior.

Houses, Hollywood, California
Architect: Helmut Schulitz
Completed 1984

Like the earlier house Schulitz designed for himself, these two houses offer spectacular views over downtown Los Angeles and the Pacific Ocean. Use of glass, however, was here restricted by energy conservation legislation. Since the views improve on the upper levels, the use of glass increases from bottom to top. The main external material is metal siding – steel on one house and natural aluminium on the other.
Unlike the Schulitz House, these houses make use of timber as both a structural and a lining material. Roof and floors are supported by proprietary composite steel and timber trusses supporting plywood decking. There is, of course, a well-established timber building tradition in California. These houses aim to demonstrate how material and labour can be saved by systematic modular coordination. The basic 42'/1200 mm module conforms to the standard size for manufactured sheet materials.

1. The main external material is silver-metal insulated siding.

2. Use of glass increases from bottom to top in order to take advantage of views.

3. The external terrace links the two houses together.

4. Steel lattice trusses again, but metal decking replaced by plywood.

House at Almere, near Amsterdam
Architects: Benthem, Crouwel
Completed 1984

This was one of ten winning designs in a competition held in 1982, the prize being free use of a site for five years. The house had to be capable of being dismantled and removed, leaving the site completely clear. The architects decided on an easily demountable construction using lightweight, low-cost, high-performance materials, which would allow the house to be relocated. Minimum space standards were also followed, which helped keep the weight of the house and the number of components to a minimum.

The single-storey plan is based on a 6.5'/2 m grid. The floor rests on a space frame supported on four concrete ground pads. The roof deck is supported mainly by the glazed walls on three sides of the plan and restrained against wind uplift by steel wires attached to the floor deck.

The architects assembled the house themselves, using it as a testing ground for components, materials, and techniques that they were proposing to use on other projects.

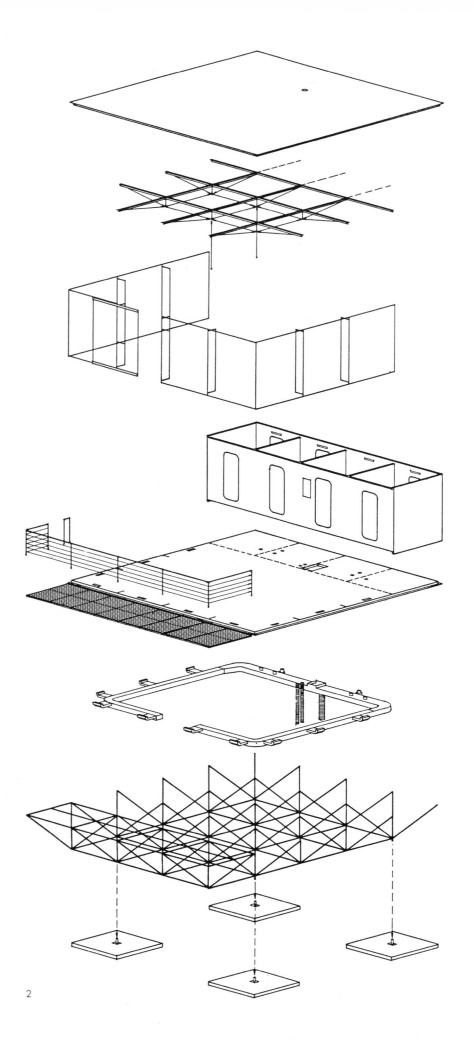

1

2

148

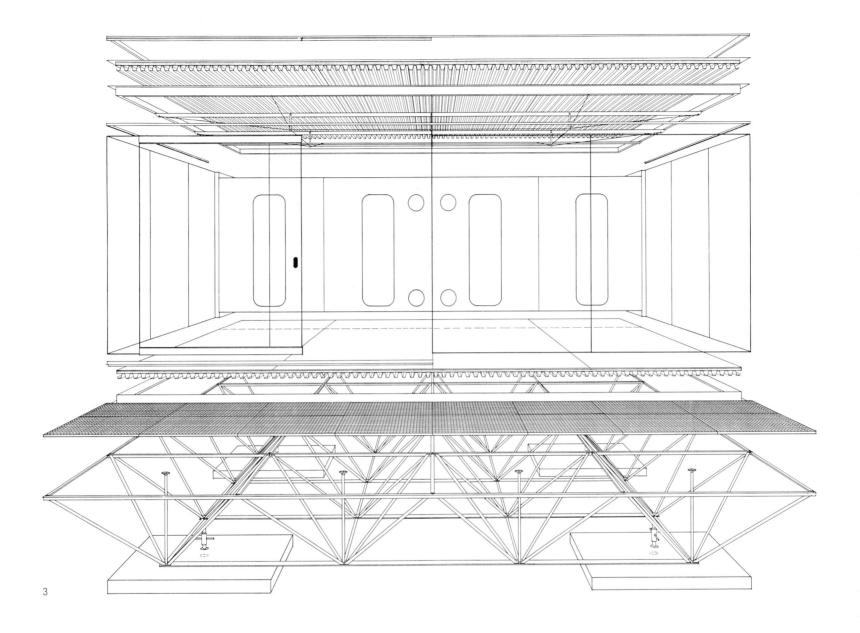

3

1. House and pylon: different function, similar expression.

2. Diagram of main building elements.

3. Exploded perspective. The roof is supported by the glass walls and held down by tension wires connected to the floor.

149

4

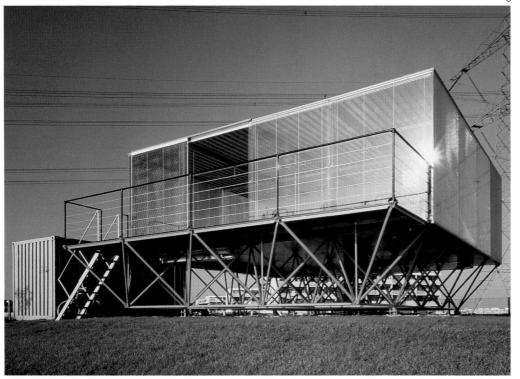

5

4. The temporary house contrasts sharply with its traditional neighbours. Privacy was not a high priority.

5. Glass and steel: the characteristic materials of High Tech.

6. All doors are hatches, as if this were a vehicle rather than a house.

6

Radio Stations, Austria
Architect: Gustav Peichl
1969 – 1981

There are radio stations, at Linz, Salzburg, Innsbruck, Dornbirn, Graz and Eisenstadt, all designed to the same brief for the Austrian Broadcasting Corporation, ORF. They were required to have efficient circulation, maximum flexibility and to be capable of extension. Each building has two wings attached radially to a two-storey circular core containing the entrance hall. The three-storey office wing, surmounted by a platform with an antenna, takes the form of a right-angled quadrant. The studios themselves take up the remaining 270 degrees of the circle. The plan is therefore a straightforward expression of the function of the building and of the requirement that each part should be extendable.

The High Tech character of the building is largely due to the silver protective coating on the precast concrete panels, the exposed air conditioning ducts clad in shiny metal, and details such as nautical handrails and railway carriage windows. The whole complex is conceived as a piece of electro-mechanical equipment.

1. Salzburg. Gleaming ductwork flanking the central staircase.

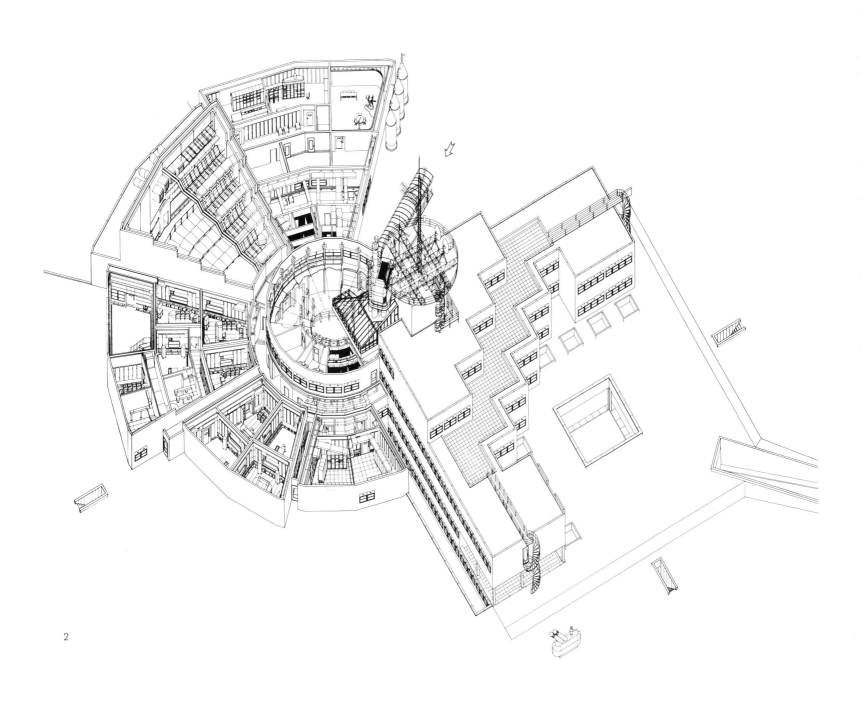

2

2. Axonometric drawing of the ORF studio in Graz.

4

5

6

3. ORF studio in Eisenstadt. The aerial tower from the roof of one of the radial wings.

6. ORF studio in Salzburg. Technical areas in the foreground, office wing to the right.

4. View of the office wing at Salzburg with aerial platform above and refrigeration vents in the foreground.

155   5. Salzburg. Central hall and staircase.

**Pavilion for travelling exhibition of IBM Europe
Architects: Renzo Piano with Shunji Ishida and
Alessandro Traldi
Completed 1984**

The IBM travelling exhibition was intended to further knowledge of computer technology, particularly among young people. It appeared for about a month in each of twenty European cities.

The brief was to provide a flexible space, something between a botanical pavilion and an exhibition gallery, in which to show a range of high technology ideas and equipment in general use.

It was essential that the interior of the pavilion in which the sensitive electronic apparatus was to be displayed should allow precise control of the microclimate and that the exhibition should always be adjustable to local conditions.

The pavilion consists of a transparent gallery which can be completely dismantled. It includes all the necessary exhibition units and showcases. Every time the pavilion is reassembled on a new site, a specific plan for its integration into the local context has to be drawn up. All the building then needs to make it work is connection to the electrical grid.

The arched superstructure is assembled from 160 individual sections and stands on a rigid base which can be adjusted to suit site levels. The three basic materials for the superstructure are: laminated beech wood for the tension and compression struts, polycarbonate for the transparent pyramids, and aluminium for the connection pieces.

1. Detail, elevation.

2., 3. Pavilion under construction in front of the Natural History Museum in London.

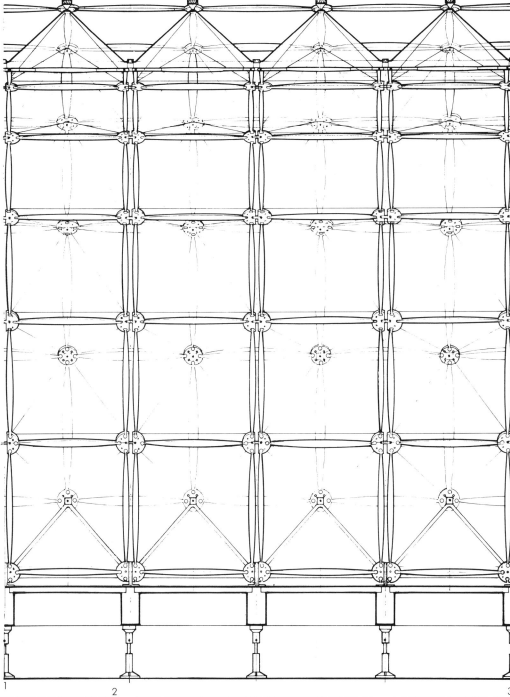

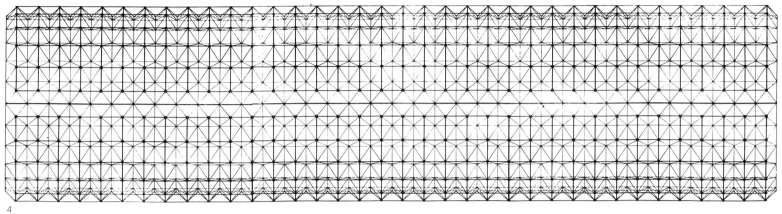

4

4. Roof plan.

5. Detail, section. A fully serviced floor with a
geodesic superstructure.

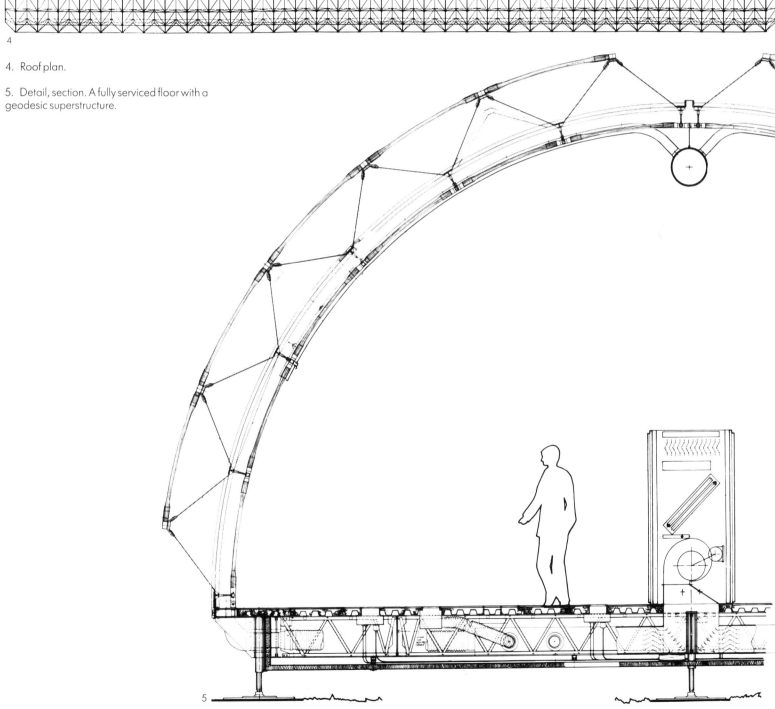

5

Index of Architects